The Answer

Proof of God in Heaven

By
Marius Forté

Written by
Sam Sorbo

TELEMACHUS PRESS

Cover designed by Telemachus Press, LLC

Cover art:
Copyright © 17958251/iStockphoto
Copyright © 3409647/iStockphoto

Interior images:
Graph of Relative Virtue and Graph of Grace by Sam Sorbo
Interior art under license from Richard Bornemann 3D Art and Animation except for Graph of Relative Virtue and Graph of Grace
Interior art uses these images licensed from iStock Photo:

Copyright © 17958251/iStockphoto	Copyright © 17943875/iStockphoto
Copyright © 562629/iStockphoto	Copyright © 16673296/iStockphoto
Copyright © 8858062/iStockphoto	Copyright © 17489020/iStockphoto
Copyright © 13825372/iStockphoto	Copyright © 17663335/iStockphoto
Copyright © 15859900/iStockphoto	Copyright © 14452654/iStockphoto
Copyright © 15517876/iStockphoto	Copyright © 16336272/iStockphoto
Copyright © 17948519/iStockphoto	Copyright © 4348253/iStockphoto
Copyright © 953426/iStockphoto	Copyright © 15706843/iStockphoto
Copyright © 14849650/iStockphoto	Copyright © 3548056/iStockphoto
Copyright © 15070933/iStockphoto	Copyright © 13588761/iStockphoto
Copyright © 15452084/iStockphot	Copyright © 25294677/iStockphoto/nabihariahi
Copyright © 15900242/iStockphoto	Copyright © 11680625/iStockphoto/danleap

Published by Telemachus Press, LLC
http://www.telemachuspress.com

Visit the author website:
http://www.theanswer-book.com

ISBN: 978-1-939337-35-1 (eBook)
ISBN: 978-1-939337-36-8 (Paperback)
ISBN: 978-1-939927-91-0 (Hardback)

Version 2013.11.19

Printed in the United States of America

10 9 8 7 6 5 4 3 2 1

"One of the best guidebooks that I've ever seen for life and its challenges. You should only get this book if you want an even happier, more fulfilling life."
—Rusty Humphries, Nationally Syndicated Radio Talk
Show Host—Talk Radio Network

"Sam is one of the toughest and most dedicated women I know … spiritually and physically. *The Answer* examines all the most intimate and important questions we humans have, regarding our lives here on earth, and it provides some intriguing and uplifting answers."
—Alice Cooper

"In an age of superficiality, Forté and Sorbo's book, *The Answer*, will challenge you to examine eternity. A well-written and thought-provoking book that will stand the test of time."
—William J. Federer, best-selling author

"Atheists won't like this book."
—Kevin Sorbo, Actor, Director, Producer

Dedication

This book is for people who are just starting or continuing their quest for the why's in this universe and its infinite mysteries. It is dedicated to those who hunger for authentic knowledge of the eternal and who take personal interest in where they come from and where they will end up. We wrote this book to honor and support those who are humbled by humanity's position in the universe and are open to being enlightened by God's infinite love so they, too, will enjoy eternal life in God's presence.

Acknowledgements

I would like to thank my good friend Sam Sorbo. This book has been my dream for as far back as I can remember. Absent Sam, I might still be talking about a book that I would write "some time." With a lot of patience and hard work, Sam made it possible for me to actually look at a finished copy of The Answer. I also must thank my parents, who gave me all their unconditional love, and honored me with a religious upbringing that instilled deeply within me a firm understanding of right and wrong, the knowledge of Christ, and what it means to be a Christian. My wife Marti and my two beautiful children, Lara and Tristan prove to me every day that miracles are possible.

—Marius Forté

My thanks go first to Marius, for conceiving of this book and entrusting me with committing it to paper, as well as to my husband, Kevin, and my kids, who put up with my writing until all hours of the night. Mark, Donna, Kaz, Caryn, and Joryn helped with their early reading of the text and their comments. Marius joins me in thanking them for their uplifting and invaluable input.

We also wish to express our profound appreciation of our gracious, loving God for His patient guidance with this project.

—Sam Sorbo

Our existence, our waking in and discovery of this universe, inexorably leads us to one particular question: Where did this all come from?

Was all this created by chance, or was it by design? Is there order or chaos? These are the two possible choices.

If the universe was designed, then there is a Creator.

If this all happened by happy accident, well, first that presumes that chance exists.

If we can prove that chance does not exist, we are left with only one correct answer.

If chance does not exist,
then everything we experience becomes evidence of the Creator.

THE ANSWER

Table of Contents

THE ANSWER

Proof of God in Heaven

Introduction

Imagine ...

No, not the beautiful melody by John Lennon.

Imagine a Universe.

Now, imagine this universe makes *complete sense*. Love rules over evil, but evil often surfaces. Imagine a place where everything you do, no matter how small and no matter how grave, regardless if it is noticed by someone, by no one, or by everyone, will return to you in exactly the same weight and proportion. Everything you send out into the universe comes back to you in equivalence. There is perfect balance for each individual and his or her actions and experiences.

Nothing is lost and nothing is forgotten.

To the infinite universe, time has little value. A day is a year is a lifetime is a moment. Imagine a world of logic, where all things are justified by eternity, not by human time. In this universe, *eventually* prevails, sooner or later ... (It doesn't care which).

Imagine, please, that the universe has a memory like an elephant's, infallible. It forgets nothing. All information is stored until its 'quality of time,' when it has ripened and is re-released into your life. There is total and absolute accountability: to yourself, to your fellow souls, and to God, of course. And what is at stake is either life eternal, or everlasting misery.

Imagine, if only for a moment, that your entire life is both assessment and testament.

All the information in your life, all of your personal data regarding your choices and decisions and all of your actions, is a test. All of your thoughts, good and bad, are witnessed and recorded like responses on a pass/fail exam. You alone will answer for your thoughts and deeds, because what you sow you shall also, inevitably, reap.

It is easy to contemplate what you might do if you were to face a certain situation. But do you *know*? If the strange turns and twists of life suddenly present you with new decisions to make and an opportunity or necessity to do, to act, to save or destroy, to stand up or fold, to follow through or turn away, will you pass or not?

Imagine a soldier at war, who was never a particular hero. A good guy, who laughed a lot and loved his fellow soldiers, but missed his family. He never knew he had heroics in him until the moment he felt the grenade hit his chest, and then saw it lying at his feet, when he threw himself on top of it to save his buddies. He gave up his most valuable possession, his life. That selfless, impulsive act is recorded in this universe. Forever.

Imagine a man who would never hurt a fly, who is righteous, honest and caring. Then one day, the thing we call coincidence bestows upon him an easy million dollars at his brother's expense. He always said he would never cheat anyone, but he secretes the money away, and then rationalizes it when he is confronted with the truth. He labels his brother, who is left penniless, an "evil-doer," although nothing could be further from the truth. Now it is clear what the man's soul has become because he failed this part of the test. This, too, is recorded, and someday there will be a reckoning.

Cause and Effect. You get what you pay for …

Imagine that every thought and every action counts, and your soul hangs in the balance. It is not the frivolous, irresponsible utopia of the song. It is a world of obvious logic and perpetual accountability. This newly imagined world is much better. It is one of freedom and responsibility, because you cannot have one without the other. This place has struggles, triumphs, failures, and true joy, because happiness must be earned to be appreciated. This is a world that makes perfect sense. Justice reigns, and compassion is the most gracious virtue.

This isn't the world that Lennon misguidedly envisioned in his beautiful song. His world was without consequences. On the surface, that might seem like the best solution, but if you follow the logic of it, his was an imagined world of pointless apathy. It was a world at peace, but remember, peace can only be valued in light of chaos. Without any defining commotion, without comparison, peace ceases to exist. Lennon dreamed of no greed or hunger. No wants or desires. In his imaginary world, there was nothing to live for or die for. There was nothing to fight for. Every one walked around with frontal lobotomies.

Our newly imagined universe is much better because responsibilities and consequences are ensured by an intractable logic. There is evil, but it can be overcome by good, which is better than no evil at all, as we can only define good or evil in light of the other. You are free to love, hate, desire, enjoy and mourn. There is strife and there are also the senses of accomplishment, loyalty, and winning. You can fight for what you believe. You must, in fact. This is the universe that makes perfect sense, a world you can depend on.

Now imagine this is the universe where you live.

The poetry of Lennon's "Imagine" is undeniably seductive, isn't it? It is a very beautiful song, a lilting and graceful use of the English language. But his song postulates a false utopia, when we have the real thing already.

I love poetry. Good poetry can transcend the boundaries of the mind, and speak directly to the soul. It gives cause for contemplation and sometimes even reverence. It uses emotion to enlighten us. I find poetry everywhere: in the falling leaves and the birds' chorus.

The most provocative natural poetry is coincidence, because it is the lyrical expression of reason. The funny thing is, coincidence does not actually exist. Once you reject the illusion of coincidence, and comprehend that nothing happens by accident, reason prevails by default.

Reason rules, cloaked in coincidence and happenstance.

Reason often prefers to remain invisible, and we humans enjoy our imaginings of luck and fate. Now, isn't that a poetic world to live in? It is a spiritual place, for certain. It is a world that welcomes all of you, your faults and your gifts, because it holds you accountable and it holds to truth. This is the place of answers.

I have had countless conversations about spirituality, my favorite subject, with people from all walks of life and from all over the globe. Having been raised in Vienna, I left when I was still a teenager and I have traveled extensively, living in Africa, Saudi Arabia, Paris and New York. Through my exchanges with poor and wealthy, educated and ignorant, Jewish, Muslim, Christian, Atheist, and Agnostic, I have learned much and taught as well. I've discovered that there are a few things on which most people agree: *the questions.*

Since man has had organized thoughts, these same fundamental questions have persisted:

- Is there a God?
- If there is a God, is He good?
- If He is good, how could He permit so much suffering?
- Is there life after death?
- What's it all about?

Some truths are self-evident, such as why a wheel should be round, instead of rectangular. Some require more in-depth reflection, like why manhole covers are always round. (Consider that for a moment. Do you know the answer?) This book intends to bring some of the less obvious truths to the foreground for inspection. We will discuss principles of science and philosophy, and show how they can also logically apply to our personal lives, relationships, and ultimately to our happiness. These ideas are not new. I am not claiming to reinvent the wheel. I am providing a closer look at the self-evident truths you may have simply accepted without a second thought, because these are the bulwarks on which you can build a lasting understanding of life.

In some ways this book is a pragmatic approach to faith. I have a friend who believes that faith is a gift, and that some people, like atheists, are simply denied that gift of faith. I strongly disagree. I believe that someone who searches for an answer can find one, and if they look hard enough to find truth, they will find faith. Even the atheist has faith in the non-existence of God. (There is no empirical proof.) After reading this book you will likely acknowledge the impossibility of the statement, "There is no God." But I am getting ahead of myself here. This book is about explanations: God, faith, love, forgiveness, hope, happiness, and reason.

There are many paths, not all of them lead in truth. But the ways of truth can also be too complicated or over-thought. I can take I-95 from Philadelphia to NY, or I can go via Chicago and Seattle. Both ways lead to my destination, but only by following misleading signposts would I take the detour. It is my sincere wish that this book clears and simplifies your path toward God and your own lasting peace and happiness.

Have you ever tried a Rubik's Cube? I admit; I found them frustrating. I could only get a short way toward the solution before I would lose momentum and make a mess of the colors again. It was hopeless for me, and frustrating. One day I saw someone perform a solution, twisting and turning the cube with lightning speed. He worked so quickly; his hands and the colors were a blur. He didn't just solve the puzzle right there, like I had been trying to do. There was a key, and he had it! He applied a series of solution patterns in a methodical manner, and suddenly, each side had only one color, when moments before, the entire cube was a mish-mash of different hues. For him, fixing a Rubik's Cube was child's play because he understood the key. But he had to discover, somehow, the patterns themselves. (Now I know there are tutorials online for this.)

Life on earth is like a Rubik's Cube to us. It is difficult and complicated; we get things wrong and sometimes make our lives worse in the process. Maybe, like me, you can get one side all blue, but the rest is still just a mish-mash of colors. The good news: There is a key. There exists a series of logical solutions, a way of evaluating, comprehending and behaving that simplifies and organizes this life, and removes the frustrating confusion and any sense of futility.

This book does not require your faith. It will not supply you with belief. Those choices are yours alone. In this book we promise simple facts that are easily understandable for anyone with a desire for knowledge and for answers. This book provides the definite solutions to the puzzle of life. Once you know the answer, it looks so easy, but if you have never been shown the key, life's mysteries may seem incomprehensible. They are not. The keys are found in the laws of the universe, which we discuss in chapter one. They may seem scientific and bland, but they are the cornerstones of great faith. From those fundamental and physical laws, you can extrapolate the philosophical and spiritual laws that govern your existence. We have tried to keep the scientific references as light as possible—who likes to read stereo instructions?—but science is essential to providing the terms we use to define ourselves and answer our most intimate questions of life and death. So, while the book starts with some basic scientific and metaphysical fundamentals, understand that those concepts underpin the whole of human life, and they are very important!

When you see the solution, it suddenly seems so evident. Manhole covers are round because any other shape could too easily fall back into the hole (and they are incredibly heavy—making retrieval very difficult.) Simple, but not obvious. This book presents the uncomplicated explanations to the ultimate riddles of life.

Chapter 1

What are the Laws of the Universe?

TRUTH

The truth is a very narrow path,
stupidity a never ending jungle.
—Johann Wolfgang von Goethe

• • • + • • • = • • • • • •

Three plus three always equals six, no matter how much one questions or debates it.

Looking at life differently …

Have you ever looked at one of those three-dimensional pictures? The kind in which, if you stare at it long enough, a 3-D image appears? I used to stare until my eyes turned red and my head swam, to no avail. Then someone explained to me that the trick is to *not* search so closely within the image for the shape, but to look *through* the picture, or look at a spot in front of the picture, and the image would form magically. I tried and eventually understood that, if I un-focused my eyes (no simple task), then a fully formed image in three dimensions would dramatically appear within the chaos of the picture I was ogling. It is an amazing transformation, though I still struggle with the visual, which has a tendency to go in and out of focus, as my eyes continue to try to readjust to the flat paper. With practice, however, it becomes easier and easier to visually lure the 3-D form from the page. This book will do that for your image of God. Once you understand the concepts of these initial chapters, God will be as obvious to you as stripes on a zebra. He may still be a bit ethereal, but as you review and familiarize yourself with the logic presented here, His existence will become a statement instead of conjecture, a 3-D vision, in spite of the two-dimensionality of these pages.

FUNDAMENTAL LAWS

Our universe reveals itself to us through absolute laws, the woven threads of the fabric of life. There are physical laws, such as gravity, that are scientifically theorized and proven. Gravity applies as a constant in our lives. You can't see it, but you have faith that gravity will continually pull you down to earth. Your faith, formed before you learned to speak, is rooted in the fact that you have never floated away. In this book, we will discuss equivalent, metaphysical laws that are more spiritual in nature, but are nonetheless scientifically indisputable. These laws are equally as faithful, constant and irrefutable as gravity and they are all intertwined, and thus you will meet them repeatedly throughout this book. They are all fundamental to understanding life, death, souls, and even God.

These simple principles are the master keys that unlock all the secrets in the universe.

BALANCE

When you press a stone, the stone presses back.
—Isaac Newton

Everything in this universe is perfectly balanced. The only element that is outside of balance is time. If a pendulum starts at thirty degrees from neutral, it takes time to swing to thirty degrees on the other side, and then time again to bring it back to its starting point. When you watch the last leaf in fall that finally drops to the ground, you would think the forest had died. But give it time, because winter is simply part of the cycle and in spring everything comes back to life again. Within the cycle of breathing in and out you find perfect harmony—balance. It's simply time-delayed. If you look at a snapshot of the moment, there appears to be an imbalance, but given time, balance always returns.

A wave, man and woman, hot and cold, good and evil, and finally, life and death. Examples of balance could fill pages, but suffice it to say that nothing exists outside of balance. It is an absolute.

There are two scientific laws that provide good examples of the law of balance. The first states that energy is never created or destroyed, only transferred from one form into another. Newton's Third Law of Motion states that any time a force acts from one object onto another, there is an equal force acting back on the original object. That means if I push you, you actually must push back and/or move away such that the total energy remains constant. Either you resist the push, meaning you are presenting me with an opposite force of pushing, or you move, which means my energy is transferred to you, because my hand will not pass through you as if you were a ghost. Put those two physical laws together and you have balance. Metaphysically, this means that whatever I 'push' out into the world is neither lost nor destroyed (like energy.) It will eventually find its way to 'push' me back. (Newton's Third Law of Motion.)

Balance is our mirror.

Remember, as a child, calling another child a name, and hearing back, "I know you are, but what am I?" That, strangely, is a very good example of the law of balance. Think of this law as a mirror. If you smile in the mirror, the mirror smiles back at you. If you raise your fist, the image in the mirror raises its fist and threatens you. Just as two plus two always equals four, everything that we pass out into the world will return to us. The sun pulls with gravity against the earth, and the earth pulls equally against the sun. Centrifugal force and inertia keeps them from colliding (thank God!), an active example of the balance that is found throughout life. The Universe demands balance, and balance is achieved, each and every time.

POLARITY

To every action there is always an equal and opposite reaction.
—Newton's Third Law of Motion

Polarity is the twin of balance. The Chinese refer to polarity as the 'yin and yang': two halves of the same circle that are interacting, or intertwined.

Polarity is balance and more. The Universe is balanced. It must be or it could not exist. In fact, everything in this life is balanced or it would not exist. A man needs a woman to create life, an exhalation follows an inhalation to sustain life, and we can breathe out nothing more than we have breathed in before. Waking follows sleeping. Events and situations are created on the backs of prior events and previous situations, although because of polarity we can only experience one pole or its opposite at any time. There is no gray area in polarity.

We can experience either life or death, but never both at once, because death is the absence of life. We can be either man or woman, but not both simultaneously. We can be awake or asleep, but not both. You can either breathe in or exhale, not both at the same time. We can have lunch at midday or we can get a midnight snack, but we cannot have midnight at noon. A light is on or it is off, a nation is at war or at peace, a calculation is either right or wrong. I am either guilty or I am innocent.

Just a little pregnant ...

Is this too black and white for you? Consider this: heat exists, but cold does not. How do we measure cold? We don't. We measure heat. Cold is simply a descriptive word, not a scientifically measureable value. Scientifically, the coldest temperature, absolute zero, negative 458° Fahrenheit or 0° Kelvin, is defined as the absence of any heat. Heat, on the other hand, is quantifiable because heat is energy. Cold is not the opposite of heat. It is the absence of it. Light is either present or there is darkness. If darkness were an entity by itself, we would be able to have more of it. But to make a room darker you must remove light, and if light is there, then you are not dealing with darkness, but simply a small degree of light. Likewise, evil is not a thing in and of itself. Evil is simply the absence of good, just as silence is the absence of noise, and you can't be just a little pregnant.

All that is necessary for the triumph of evil is that good men do nothing.
—Edmund Burke

The sister of polarity is balance, because balance defines the poles. Roger Federer cannot play tennis against a beginner, and conversely it takes a Raphael Nadal to define the greatness of Federer. Without the positive there is not a negative; there is nothingness.

The universe combines polarities in a continuous sequence and that is how this material world exists, each pole in sequence, delineated by time or otherwise. Is it daytime or nighttime? It is both in sequence. Are we in wartime or do we have peace? Both, in succession. What goes up must come down, in sequence. It cannot be both up and down simultaneously. He was innocent until he became guilty. The wave is high and then it is low. The crest balances the trough, spring balances against fall, in sequence, and north balances against south. Without one the other would cease to exist.

Every outside has an inside and every inside has an outside, and though they differ, they are a matched set.

The world turns. If it stopped, one side would burn in flames and the other would freeze. Each side is the polar opposite to the other side with respect to the sun. If you only breathe in, your life would soon fade. Remove the positive current from the light bulb, and the room goes dark. The bulb needs both poles to conduct electricity, each on an opposing side, in sequence.

This world contains both sides of polarity, but, as humans, we are destined to experience most of them in sequence, instead of simultaneously. The earth has both the North and South Poles, but we can only be at one or the other of them at a time.

Every coin has two sides.

CAUSE AND EFFECT

Whatever you sow, you shall reap.
—Jesus Christ

First we sow, and then we reap. It is a process that is time-delayed. Christ said "whatever," meaning everything, not quite a bit, or some.

The law of cause and effect is so pervasive that it is easily overlooked. If a tree falls in the forest, it crushes the things it falls on (even if no one is there to hear it). Nothing happens in a vacuum, but luckily we don't live in a vacuum. Every action predicates its effect, and for every effect there is a preceding action.

This is common sense, but strangely enough, most people do not appreciate that this law applies on the metaphysical plane. By metaphysical we are referring to beyond the physical into the spiritual. Metaphysical laws apply to our lives as completely as the physical laws, and this law of cause and effect is both.

The year of 1988 builds entirely on the year before. I cannot expect to play tennis unless I've made the decision to learn to play. It is my decision to take lessons that creates the future tennis player in me. It is always the cause first, then the effect. And therefore the effect can never stand alone, because it is only through the cause that the effect finds realization.

If I see an ordinary drinking glass, this glass tells me one certainty: Before the glass came to be, there was the thought of the glass. This thought cannot be measured or weighed. It is pure spirit. But without a formulating idea, the glass would not exist. Where there is a son, there must be a father. If there is a father, there must be a son or a daughter. One bears witness to the other. If I want to grow corn, I must plant the seeds for corn. In order to lose weight, I must exercise, eat less, or both. To have a fire in the fireplace, I need to chop some wood.

Without cause and effect, there is nothing. Think about it, everything is a result of something else that came before. The opposite is also true.

Any creation bears witness to its creator, absolutely.

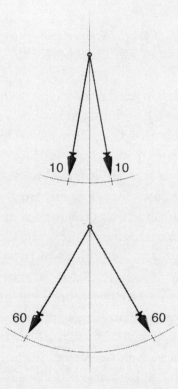

*A pendulum raised to 60 degrees will swing to the opposite side an equivalent
60 degrees, and only then swing back to return to its original starting position.
Once in motion, our actions cannot be recalled,
and the consequences are assured.*

CYCLES

In all things there is a law of cycles.
—Publius Cornelius Tacitus

Cycles are everywhere: day to night to day again, winter to spring, to summer, to fall and back to winter. The year is a cycle. All of life is a cycle. In this Universe, there are no half circles. Complete circles, cycles, abound. A clock is a half-day cycle, as all time is cyclical. That is why clocks are round. The second sweeps the full circumference of the clock face. The minute and hour hands do the same, because the sun rises, sets, then rises again. Over and over. Your blood circulates throughout your body, always returning to the heart, its motivating force. Adults give birth to babies, who in turn grow up to be adults and have children, starting the cycle again. Water circulates into the air by evaporation into clouds, into rain and snow by condensation, and back into the oceans and rivers by gravity. Which came first, the chicken or the egg? We don't know, because all of this life is an endless cycle. Sleeping and waking follow the same principle. It's not about precedence, because everything is cyclical. You inhale; you exhale; you start the cycle again.

If you cannot define it as a complete cycle then you have not considered the whole of it.

Some might argue that the law of gravity is more important in this case than the cycle, and they would be correct if we were only contemplating the here and now. The gravitational pull of the sun forces the earth to circle it. Only a great external force could prevent the sun from 'rising' tomorrow morning. We have faith that it will rise because anything else would be extraordinary. It would be out of the pattern, or the cycle, that has been established and that we use to define our daily lives.

By law of periodical repetition, everything which has happened
once must happen again and again—and not capriciously,
but at regular periods, and each thing in its own period,
not another's, and each obeying its own law.
–Mark Twain

Here on Earth, the law of gravity is a rational law, and the law of cycles is an abstract one. By this, I mean that gravity is both a confirmed constant and an empirical law, proven by science and therefore accepted as fact (although scientific fact has been known to change substantially after further research!). The law of cycles is also constant, and for our purposes, it is more relevant than gravity. The law of cycles, as applied to gravity (and many other empirical laws), means that gravity exists, and has the same effect on all things at all times. It doesn't take Thursdays off. It isn't less effective on holidays. That's the definition of a constant and also the effect of a full cycle.

What goes up must come down.

Even the economy is cyclical. There is no rational explanation for it (aside from human greed getting us into trouble, repeatedly,) but that it also is subject to the law of cycles.

Those who do not learn from history are doomed to repeat it.

It seems more like we are simply doomed to not learn from history. The application of the law of cycles is more extensive than popular culture admits. For example, once you are born, one fact is assured: you will die. If you extend the Law of Cycles through its logical paces, then things cannot end there. Death completes only half the cycle, but half-cycles simply do not exist. We must be missing the other half of that picture—what happens after death.

We have confidence that day will follow night. How do we know it will? Experience? Of course. Scientific evidence? Yes. Faith? Meteors exist and the stars burn out, so, yes, even a little bit of faith, too. And that (involuntary) faith is reliant on the law of cycles.

RESONANCE

Nie könnte das Auge die Sonne erblicken, wäre es nicht sonnenhaft.
The eye can only see the sun because it was designed to see the sun.
—Johann Wolfgang von Goethe

In this one sentence, Goethe summarized the Law of Resonance. You cannot receive a radio station on AM if the dial is on FM. And unless you turn to exactly the correct wavelength, you won't hear a thing from that station. I cannot read Voltaire unless I know French, nor can I express beauty if I have none in myself. I can only express something outwardly if I have it created it first within myself. Seeing a piece of art that is threatening, dark and negative tells a great deal about the artist who created it. Likewise, the person who enjoys that type of art does so because the image resonates in him, and finds purchase within his emotions. Misery loves company.

Have you ever shone a flashlight in the dark? What does it do, unless it shines on something that resonates and reflects? It's just a useless shaft of nothingness. The purpose of the flashlight is to shine on things. Those are the resonant articles the flashlight was intended to illuminate.

If a tree falls in the woods, and no one sees it, did it really fall?

It did, once it was observed. A film in a canister is nothing without the projector and screen, which then use resonance to fulfill the purpose of the film. Likewise, the screen and projector have little value without the film. A computer without its software or the software without a computer would each be equally useless. Have you written the greatest novel of all time? It is meaningless, unless people read it. Would Beethoven have written anything if he didn't believe it would find resonance with an audience? When a joke is told, one person with a developed sense of humor gets the joke, but the other person demands an explanation; because for him, the humor has no resonance.

A surgeon needs patients, or his years of training are wasted. The pen is made for the paper and an ear is designed to hear sound. Female sexual organs are specifically designed to receive the male's. One is specifically made for the other.

In order for us to experience love, we must love *something*. That something is the resonant object of our affection. You cannot love nothing; love demands an object on which to be focused; light a spotlight, like a flashlight in the dark.

These laws exist in a God-inspired cosmic explosion and create all the possibilities of what we call life. Life can only exist because of these intertwining laws, which are as evident as gravity.

LAWS IN ACTION

The whole of science is nothing more
than a refinement of everyday thinking.
—Albert Einstein[1]

I once lived next door to an empty lot, and a friend came to visit. When he came back a year later, there was a house on the once-vacant lot! Now, my friend, an evolutionist, quickly claimed that this house miraculously evolved. I patiently explained that an architect designed and built the house. Cause and Effect.

Nothing comes from nothing.

Something can only come from something. A one cannot come out of a zero.

"Did you *see* the architect? Have you spoken to him?" he asked me. I shook my head. Having no proof of the existence of an architect, he said he could not possibly believe that a "creator" made the house. Most of us would agree that his obstinacy was naïve, but this naïveté is commonplace when it comes to our ultimate creator.

Like gravity, which works as well on Monday as it does on Thursday, even if it is your birthday, the laws of the universe are ubiquitous. You can attack them, deny them, or ignore them, but they are there and they apply, regardless of your feelings. Once you understand and respect them, they can be used to further your appreciation of the universe and of God, who is the master creator, as the laws of the universe prove.

It seems self-evident that if there is no precedence for any ordered creation to spring from the chaos of this world, a human being, with the spark of a soul (the most complex of inventions), could not just evolve from the mud. Is there so little difference between the living and non-living that it was an accident when the first living cell began? My wife was pregnant; why didn't she give birth to a tractor?

The cosmic watchmaker is watching.

Some people argue that a watch is no proof of a watchmaker. They postulate, for instance, that my home's electricity comes from the electric company, but lightning, which is also electricity, does not. The electric company clearly is not responsible for all known electricity. But just because there is a clear creator for one type of electricity cannot exclude the notion that the other kind would not have its own creator. Cause and Effect would argue that. Just because my home's electricity is ordered and controlled does not imply that lightning is not, and therefore has no creator. It is impudent and presumptuous to assume that because something *appears* random, it has no organizing force, or watchmaker. We review "entropy" in the next chapter. Just because wood grows as a tree, does not imply that the wood in the table grew as a table. Of course not, for the table there was a distinct craftsman. But for the tree, as for the lightning, there was one as well, though less apparent.

Cause and Effect, Balance, Polarity, and Cycles work together in Resonance to create this structure of our universe, like a great pillow on which we can lie down and know we are safe. This set of laws is the unimpeachable, unflagging evidence that there is order in the chaos we experience as life, the bulwarks on which every theory about creation may be tested and proven. Because these principles are as much spiritual as they are physical, they function like the memory of the universe. The pendulum never fails to swing back; the cycle always completes its journey. The Universe never forgets.

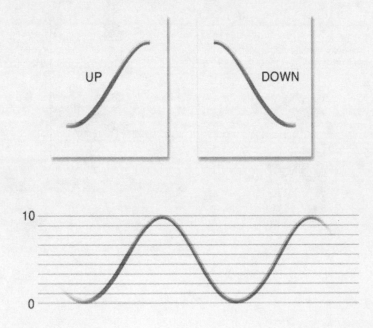

A wave is only in perfect balance if seen and experienced in a continuous movement. If we watch only a part or half of it, it seems unbalanced.

Everything in the universe can only exist
if it is in perfect balance

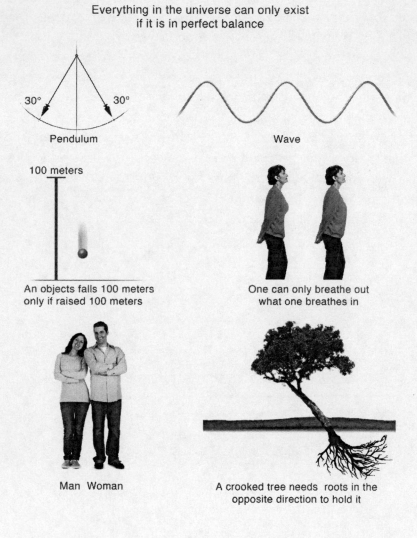

30°   30°

Pendulum   Wave

100 meters

An objects falls 100 meters   One can only breathe out
only if raised 100 meters   what one breathes in

Man Woman   A crooked tree needs roots in the
                              opposite direction to hold it

Chapter 2

Who Created the Universe (and its Laws)?

Miracles are not contrary to nature,
but only contrary to what we know about nature.
—Saint Augustine

So ... who, or what, created those immutable laws?

The second law of thermodynamics states that entropy of an isolated system that is not in equilibrium will increase over time. In laymen's terms: order is naturally and continually deteriorating into chaos. In plain English: things have a tendency to fall apart, rather than to organize themselves. (That's why moms say things like, "This house isn't going to clean itself!")

There are considerable implications with this law. First, if the Universe is constantly losing usable energy and never gaining, we must conclude the Universe is not eternal. At its beginning, the Universe was in an ordered state. The Universe had a finite beginning—the moment at which it was at 'zero entropy' (its most ordered possible state). The, after a big bang, it began winding down, like a clock. But who wound up the clock?

Many theologians reflect that while they are generally happy to discover that the Universe had a beginning, astronomers (scientists) are more upset, because the evidence then points to a clock-maker, or God.

Astronomer Robert Jastrow commented, "For the scientist who has lived by his faith in the power of reason, the story ends like a bad dream. He has scaled the mountains of ignorance; he is about to conquer the highest peak; as he pulls himself over the final rock, he is greeted by a band of theologians who have been sitting there for centuries." [2]

ENTROPY

In 1964, NASA decided it needed a life-detection system for the upcoming space mission to Mars. The scientists charged with this task wondered how Martian life could possibly reveal itself to tests established for Earthly life. To them, the basic question was how best can life be recognized? What does one look for, in looking for a life form? Their simplest answer was to look for an *entropy reduction*, since organization must be a general characteristic of life. In other words, the creation of life is actually a reversal of the second law of thermodynamics, the opposite of "natural."

If a reduction or a reversal of entropy is indicative of life, while the second law of thermodynamics states that entropy is a naturally occurring and pervasive phenomenon, meaning that order is *not* organically occurring, did the universe accidentally reverse that law and create human beings? The obvious answer is "no." The logical conclusion must be that an organized collection of something (cells, for instance) derives from an outside energy imposing a design, suppressing and prevailing over nature's predilection for chaos. Some external force must have acted to reverse the Law of Entropy and create order from disorder.

That's a big order, for order.

THE BIG BANG

Science without religion is lame,
Religion without science is blind.
—Albert Einstein[3]

The current prevailing theory of the creation of the universe is called The Big Bang Theory. In fact, there is no other widely known or accepted scientific theory. The Big Bang was developed in part because of observations made by Edwin Hubble in the 1920's. He measured the speed at which neighboring galaxies were moving away from our own. He looked all around us and found the same thing; the galaxies that were farther away moved away even faster. If we could reverse time, everything would be converging to a single point, a "singularity." Over the following decades, through experimentation and observation, scientists developed the Big Bang theory, which states that the Universe began as a single speck, at one moment, probably about fourteen billion years ago, with a—BIG BANG. No one was around to hear it, but that's the answer to a different question.

There are myriad calculations that went into identifying and reaffirming the Big Bang theory, and it is the closest we may ever get to scientifically answering the question, "How did the universe get here?" Although the laws of physics break down right *at* the singularity, scientists have determined the speed of the explosion immediately after detonation. After one tenth of a millionth of a millionth of a millionth of a millionth of a millionth of a millionth of a millionth of a second, they know precisely at what speed the universe was expanding. (They are nothing if not precise.) More importantly, they understand the critical nature of that figure. In his book, A Brief History of Time, Steven Hawking, the renowned theoretical physicist writes:

*Why did the universe start out with so nearly the critical rate of
expansion that separates models that re-collapse from those that go
on expanding forever, that even now, ten thousand million years
later, it is still expanding at nearly the critical rate? If the rate of
expansion one second after the Big Bang had been smaller by even
one part in 100 thousand million million, the universe would have
re-collapsed before it ever reached its present size.[4]*

The universe began with so precisely the critical rate of expansion that when scientists mathematically experimented with
other expansion values, the models either collapsed upon themselves or continued expanding forever. A reduction in the velocity
of expansion after the Big Bang of even one part in 100 thousand
million would not have produced our solar system, much less our
planet. The opposite is also true: if the initial explosion happened
at a greater speed by even one part in a million, stars and planets
would not have formed. But even thousands of years later, we are
still maintaining critical speed.

This kind of serendipitous accident or lucky coincidence
is repeated in many of the physical constants that apply today:
gravitational force, nuclear force, speed of light, and electromag-
netic constants. There are fifteen different quantifiable values
that current theory is unable to predict, but without which, the
formation of this universe would not have occurred. Fifteen, all
working together to create Mother Universe. This gives us the
Anthropic Principle:

**Our universe is uniquely adapted
to support human development.**

CHANCE

Chance is a myth.

Go to the casino, and place a bet on red at the roulette wheel. Assuming the wheel is balanced, you have a 50 percent chance that red will come up. The first time, maybe red comes. The second time, it is possible red comes again. Do this 100,000 times, though, and your bet of red will win about 50,000 times.

If you can back away from the situation and see it in its entirety, there is no chance. The more times you repeat the experiment, the more you will prove the 50 percent rule. Makes you wonder why people gamble, huh? It is because when you only look at the single bet, it *appears* to be governed by chance. The same logic applies to car accidents. Insurance companies, in essence, take the singular, personal, chance of your car crash out of the equation by plugging you into a larger equation with many other drivers. Suddenly, your car crash becomes *statistical*. Being the single driver makes it *seem* like your car crash is governed by luck, because that is all your limited perspective allows you to see. But being a statistic reveals the inevitability of general circumstances, and the deceptiveness of chance. Look at it this way; it isn't 'luck' that makes insurance a lucrative business. The actuaries know exactly what they're doing.

Statistics are created based on the past, but they project reliably into the future.

Our past predicts our future.

To the insurance company, the man who dies 22 years from now fulfills the prediction of the statistics of the past, removing chance from any equation. The farther from the specifics you are, the smaller role chance *appears* to play in the events. Go out to God (infinity) and there is no such thing as chance.

A doctor tells his patient the mortality rate of a certain operation is one percent. The patient answers, "But if I die, it's 100 percent."

Have you ever seen *Romeo and Juliet?* Have you ever read any Shakespearean plays? Would you ever in your wildest imagination believe that they were written by accident, that no one and nothing sat down and wrote word after word and line after line, with the plot turns, the surprise endings, the humor and wit and the moral lessons? Of course not. Words do not just magically appear by accident, or chance. If this were possible in any way, then one play, even just one, would have written itself at some point in time. All the necessary ingredients are there. I leave my computer running when I walk off to the bathroom, but chance does not come in and write some more lines in this book. It sounds silly to even consider this hypothesis, but people are somehow willing to believe that chance had a hand in the creation of this universe and all of its living creatures, which are vastly more complex, even in just one heart beat, than all of Shakespeare's plays put together. Some people are convinced that, if the time frame is long enough (given enough 'chance'), life can create itself. Yes, and no one would ever need to write a book, or make a movie, because they would just create themselves. Who needs Shakespeare when we've got Chance?

Chance is part of the great illusion of life. Think about that for a moment. Chance is the description we apply to a single event and its outcome, because we are limited in our perspective such that we can only observe single events at close-up range.

If there was any validity to the theory of chance, then chance would have worked at least once somewhere. Suppose the technicians at NASA are working on a new satellite, and they have some challenges with the design, so they decide to wait it out, because they are convinced that eventually chance will solve the problem and fix the satellite. Of course, the taxpayers would demand they be fired, and rightly so. If chance could, why has it never just built an entire satellite from nothing, or a house? Could it have created life and souls and love?

Chance is a crutch that we use to avoid Truth.

For some, the more complicated the endeavor, the easier it seems to believe that chance plays a part. Chance has never accomplished anything, because it is only an illusion.

Chance is a distraction.

"Bad luck" is the surrogate for any kind of blame. It shifts focus from the reaction to an event, and returns focus to the event itself, which is already part of the past and not part of the solution. Do not look to chance to solve any problems or create anything.

Chance is the poor man's excuse for becoming a statistic.

If chance actually existed it would supersede any law of cause and effect. Cause and effect is the meta-equivalent of gravity. It is always on. For every action there is an equal and opposite reaction. Because everything is governed by the law of cause and effect, chance has no place, and cannot claim any power. The two are mutually exclusive.

Either this universe was created by "chance," just like that, without reason or purpose, or it follows a plan. If it does follow a plan, then true to the law of cause and effect, the plan has a creator. In fact, the odds *against* our universe forming as it had, and supporting life as we know it, are truly insurmountable, which indicates that someone or something imposed some sort of design over the event.

At least whoever it was had a sense of flair.

Given this extraordinary event (may I call it a miracle?), we must ask ourselves: What came before? Unfortunately, science cannot provide a definitive answer to that, and so we are left with two choices: nothing, or God. If your answer is nothing, well, that is pretty sad, but I suppose you'll 'live.' Just remember, nothing comes from nothing.

$$0 + 0 = 0$$

Always. But if the answer is *something*, then that something is beyond the boundaries of time, space, and matter. That's a pretty astonishing something!

Consider for a moment how preposterous the idea of the Big Bang is. I mean, everything we know today, everything we are, started as a singularity? A minute point with no dimension and no mass gave birth to this? That fanciful theory, relying entirely on chance, is not really more believable than the one in which some immense power crafts the universe with His 'bare hands' in seven days.

There are those who challenge the validity of the Big Bang, relying on more recent data collected from the universe that is not widely accepted or even acknowledged by the greater scientific community. (In fact, the scientific community is easily as politically charged as many believe the religious community is.) One thing I know for certain is that modern science is constantly changing. It seems every decade or so a new theory replaces an old one as we improve our data collecting and analysis. For instance, it used to be wildly popular, even within the medical community, to smoke. Joke's on all of us. Look at "Global Warming." Whoops! I meant "Climate Change." A few decades ago it was called "Global Cooling" and we were warned that a new ice age was upon us. I suppose when we consider our sources (scientists versus theologians,) we are simply more socially programmed to rely on science. But is the Big Bang Theory really all that reassuring? And in as much as this theory, so heavily dependent on chance, does not rule out the existence of God, how does it change our experience of life? In our efforts to determine the origins of the universe, modern science is not necessarily our most reliable source.

In any creative process, was chance the creator? Did it even play a part? If an engineer struggles to design a bridge, does he say, "I hope by chance I'll solve this problem?" On the contrary, the engineer brags about having "left nothing to chance."

Yet, the greatest of all creations, the Universe, was supposedly created by chance. How silly. If other smaller creative endeavors exclude chance, how is it that seemingly smart people credit chance as the creator of the most complex and infinitely complicated thing, life itself?

Two answers: ignorance and arrogance.

EVOLUTION

I was a young man with uninformed ideas.
I threw out queries, suggestions, wondering all the time over everything;
and to my astonishment the ideas took like wild fire.
People made a religion of them.
—Charles Darwin

The Theory of Evolution has unfortunately caused great conflict between science and religion. It is mainly the result of people jumping to conclusions. Initially, Darwin wrote his theories about evolution with very little empirical evidence. He published them reluctantly because he was a sometime-believer in God and he understood the ramifications his conjecture might have for people who typically took a purely literal interpretation of the book of Genesis. Since Darwin's time, much has been proven about his theories, and, as more proof was offered, many religious types ran the other way, afraid of scientific explanations for things otherwise attributed to God. That kind of philosophy is called a "God of the gaps" philosophy, and it has intrinsic weaknesses, because gaps get filled. As more proof is offered for circumstances otherwise ascribed to God, well, His credit goes down. With regard to creation, many interpret the Bible as though God intentionally and specifically created one man, Adam, and one woman, Eve. When those two were expelled from the Garden of Eden, they joined up with other humans, and so we are left to wonder the significance of there being other humans that were created differently, or, at least, separately.

The principle argument against this literal interpretation of the Bible is that it really does not make logical sense. A good portion of the Old Testament simply cannot be accepted literally, nor was it meant to be. The Old Testament is, in places, only poetic description. For instance, in Genesis God created the sun on the third day. How can this be? There is no "day" for us that begins without some kind of sunrise. So how were the first two days delineated?

The word day can mean a literal 24-hour period, but it can also refer to a block of time. Someone saying "in my father's day" would mean "back in the 1950s," instead of implying that their father had literally lived only for one day. By this reasoning, God created different things on different "days," but perhaps it took longer than what a week is to you and me.

An admission of the validity of the theory of evolution by no means precludes the existence of a loving God. Believing in God can easily be reconciled with our scientific discoveries about our planet and our own creation. What we have discovered through genetic research is that all animals are undoubtedly related. Either that, or we have a God who is toying with us, trying to fake us out. The evidence for evolution, both micro (meaning tiny changes in genetic make-up) and macro (grand genetic changes that leap even from one species to another), is overwhelming. The fossils that have been discovered also enhance the argument for evolution, though they are not as conclusive as many would hope. But since the mapping of the human genome and the resulting discoveries regarding other animals' genes, there is little doubt in the scientific community of the *process* of evolution.

Is God evolution?

To reconcile evolution with God's plan, may we not assume that evolution *is* God's plan? If God is omnipotent, and He created the Big Bang, He clearly exists outside of time. He is present, past, and future. He is timeless. What point could there possibly be in tracking time within eternity? The fact that a day might be a 24-hour period, or an eon, certainly supports the idea that for God, time is trivial, non-existent. God was before, and is enduring for always. Since He created the earth and all its inhabitants, He created "evolution," of course.

The Theory of Evolution as the alternative to 'faith.'

I used to drive a Ford Explorer. It was a good car, but then Ford created a better one. Why? Evolution. The designers at Ford discovered that there was room for improvement in my Explorer, so they redesigned the engine and the body, and ordered different colors of leather for the seats, and the car evolved. You simply cannot discount the designers' input in improving the car. Someone thought about adding a cup-holder on the door. Pressures of the market prompted the redesign, but the designers did the work. The car did not improve itself. (Would that it could! My mechanic would be out of a job.) Not once did a Ford Explorer either go back to knock on the factory door to request an improved part or simply morph into a better version by itself. A designer crafted the enhancement and implemented it, according to an overriding plan, and not by chance.

To suppose that the eye with all its inimitable contrivances
for adjusting the focus to different distances, for admitting
different amounts of light, and for the correction of spherical
and chromatic aberration, could have been formed by natural
selection, seems, I confess, absurd in the highest degree.
—Charles Darwin

Evolution as a theory cannot be disproved. (In fairness, though, neither can God.) If seen objectively and not at too close a range, evolution grants to all non-believers an alternative to faith. This is an illustration of the free choice with which our Creator endowed us. Of course there must be an alternate choice of belief that seemingly precludes a belief in God. God is a gentleman and lives by His word. If there were no competing theories of creation, we would all just involuntarily believe in God (as many used to do.) But with science came a creativity even He might admire, and more choices for his children. If you were bamboozled by the Theory of Evolution as a replacement for a belief in God, do not be embarrassed. He created it, so, naturally, it is a brilliant ruse.

MORAL LAW

There is another law that the famous author C.S. Lewis used as evidence of the existence of God: The Moral Law. The Moral Law is the intrinsic ability of humans to determine good from bad, right from wrong, just from unjust. It is evident when children proclaim, "That's not fair!" when given less candy than their playmate. Nobody has coached them; they have an inborn, intrinsic understanding of what is reasonable and good, and what is not. In fact, this seems to be universal in humanity, and perhaps peculiar to it, as well. Other types of animals rarely exhibit anything resembling a morality. Generation upon generation of most of the earth's civilizations have had a strong pull toward belief in a spiritual being, thus the great promulgation of world religions. We are inextricably, but not inexplicably, drawn toward God. That is where we clearly see that beyond the living and breathing, there is spirit. No amount of evolution or chance can account for why humans have spirit, The Moral Law, and the desire to find God.

What is love?

People argue that they cannot feel God or see him. Can you see or feel love? How can love exist if you cannot see it or tangibly feel it? You cannot prove a feeling, but you know it is there. It exerts an overwhelming pressure on you and your behavior, and it puts a smile on your face.

> *Falling in love is not at all the most stupid thing that people do—*
> *but gravitation cannot be held responsible for it.*
> *—Albert Einstein*[5]

There was a recent news story about a father who attacked a grizzly bear that was mauling his grown son. The father used a compound bow—as a club—to beat the 800-pound beast on the head and back. What would compel an intelligent adult man to risk his life in this way? Love. To maintain that something does not exist because it is intangible is to deny the existence of love itself, an ethereal force that moves us definitively. We know that love exists as a force of nature; just as we know that, so does a loving God.

Mind over matter.
Mind before matter.

I have a wineglass. It is an ordered, designed object. That tells me one thing for certain: before the glass, there was the *thought of the glass*. This thought or idea is purely spirit. It cannot be weighed or measured. Even should the glass shatter, the thought of the glass survives because it preceded the creation of the glass. The ultimate question is where did the thought come from? Our best answer is "not from nothing." Nothing comes from nothing, and something comes only from the thought, or spirit, the non-materialistic energy of a craftsman or creator. The best name we have for that energy is God.

- Cause and effect
- Balance
- Polarity
- Cycles
- Rhythm
- Reversing entropy

- Evolution as God's plan
- Moral Law
- Chance does not exist
- What is Love?
- Mind before matter

I hope at this point it is clear that, just as houses do not pop up out of thin air, and humans do not give birth to lampshades or even giraffes, living beings did not just spontaneously appear in the muck and mire, without some external force acting upon them, crafting them out of chaos. We like to call that creative force "God."

$$0 = 0 = 0$$
$$1 + 0 = 1$$

The only way to have a 'one' is to begin with one. That is what we call the oneness of God.

*If God does not exist, why do you **care**?*

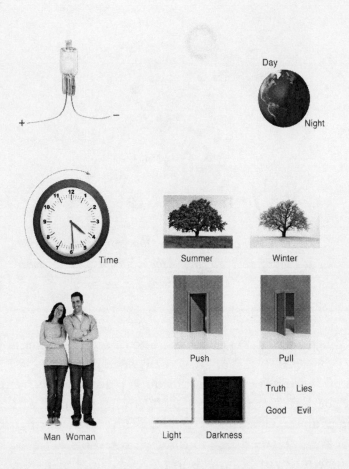

Disconnect the + wire from the bulb and the light goes out. Stop the rotation of the earth and one side will freeze while the other side burns. You can only open a door when it is closed. You can only breathe out from an inhalation. Take the woman from the man and life stops—it takes both sexes to procreate.

The right could not be the right if there were nothing left.

Chapter 3

Do Time and Matter Exist?

Great men are they who see that spiritual is stronger
than any material force—that thoughts rule the world.
—Ralph Waldo Emerson

When astronomers look out into space at a supernova in the Andromeda Galaxy, they are actually seeing into the past. They are currently witnessing an event that took place over two million years ago. The light traveling at 186,000 miles per second is certainly not instantaneous at such a distance. In fact, the farther into space we look, the further back in time we see. This ultimately signifies that time (not just beauty), is in the eye of the beholder. Our view is dependent on the light we see, and that light is different for each observer. Especially at greater distances, events in our universe are entirely observer-dependent. In laymen's terms: it's all in your unique head!

Life is deception.

In Hinduism the material world is known as *Maya*. Maya is considered to be an illusion. It is deception, and that is truly what this life is. To take a photo we generate a negative. In this life we are creating the negative that will "print out" as our souls once we pass over into death.

Time appears to us linearly. We see time as a progression of seconds and minutes, hours, days and years. If you read a book, you read one page at a time, but the book's final page is already written, even though you are not ready to read it. You only read the last page once you have read the pages before (unless you cheat and skip to the end.) Reading, like your life, is a linear process. To us, life is comprised of past, present and future, in sequence. We only understand life in these terms. But our *perception* of time does not define the way time *really* is. A child looks at a mouse and sees he is enormous by comparison. But his father, who is three feet taller, gives him a new perspective on his own size. Everything is relative.

RELATIVITY

Divine numbers are not of this world.

Is a minute long? Is a New York minute longer or shorter than a Greenwich Mean Time minute? Is a mile short? Is a building tall?

It's all relative, as they say. As humans, we are very limited in our understanding of the whole. Have you ever heard a dog whistle? No, because dog whistles are meant for dogs, and human ears cannot perceive them. But dogs hear them quite well.

Apply this reasoning to our comprehension of time, and our comprehension of the universe. As humans we are limited. We see and grasp, at best, the smallest slice of the whole. We understand that one second is short and 80 years appears long to us. The number 5, IV, or ↯↯↯ is easy to comprehend, yet the number 100,000,000 is much more difficult to grasp even though we have symbols to express both.

Jewish history is approximately 4000 years old. Christ lived 2000 years ago. This Universe is about 14 billion years old. Numbers that get too large baffle us. Time is infinitely longer than anything we can comprehend. In the spiritual sense, all numbers are one.

If someone states that six billion people is a lot of souls and he asks where they all come from, that simply shows that the Universe and its message has not reached him yet. Thinking in limited ways will limit you and keep you from understanding eternity. If we want to understand the whole picture, we have to adapt mentally to eternity. We have to adjust to an eternal plane. You would not measure the distance from Paris to New York in millimeters, for example, and you cannot measure the distance between two solar systems in miles, either. We use light-years. You must choose an appropriate yardstick, the right unit of measurement. You cannot prepare for sensitive brain surgery using a knife and fork and a bucket of marbles. To measure eternity, you must mentally adjust to an eternal plane, and all your current points of reference are no longer applicable.

Imagine the biggest ONE you've ever seen, only bigger—infinitely big. But still One.

So we apply and adapt our measuring units accordingly. For the purposes of our discussion, a million is as much as one. A billion is as much as one. The ONE-NESS of God, and being one with God, is life in a different dimension, and yet it is truer than any reality we experience in this life.

Christ died one death for us, but the 'us' is all of us.

Although we haven't addressed Christ in this book yet, He provides a great example of spiritual numbers versus material ones. On simply the physical plane Christ would have needed to have died an infinite number of deaths, over and over again, a single death for each and every one of us. He died His single death *for one and for all*. For eternity. So a ONE becomes equivalent to a BILLION and

more. And once that BILLION becomes like Christ, they will find
the ONENESS with God. Christ is the point at the peak of the
cone, with no physical dimension, and we are the base of the cone,
on a physical plane in the dimensions of time and space.

Numbers have no volume. Time has no dimension.

TIME

As if you could kill time without injuring eternity.
–Henry David Thoreau

Time has three dimensions: past, present and future. The only
way we can experience our life is through the present moment,
with knowledge of the past and an expectation of the future. I
know one certain thing, and that is that I only have the present
moment. You cannot go into the future and pull the future into
the present. Not even five or ten seconds of it. From your present
moment, the future, no matter how close it is, cannot yet be
attained. Similarly, the past is also beyond your reach. You can
never rework it or relive it. You can never go back. You only own
this moment, this 'now.'

There is a film projector for the movie of your life. Time is
the mechanism by which you can view your motion picture. The
entire film exists already in the celluloid, and it sits, waiting for
the machine to reel it through and reveal to you each momentary
photo, in sequence and in timing to make it look authentic, like a
moving picture. Your entire story from beginning to end, resides
already in the film, but your requirement is to see each moment as it
comes. You can only access the tale through the use of a projector,
frame by frame.

Everyone gets to the future in the same time.

In actuality, the present moment has no dimension, because it only 'is.' The common phrase, "a point in time" sums it up nicely. A point has no dimension. In mathematics a point is a dimensionless spot, a position. It can be located, but it cannot be measured. A mathematical point has no height, width, or length. Similarly, a point in time, a moment, 'now,' also has no dimension. Gone already, once you encounter it. And gone again. And gone again. I have the present moment but I do not, really, because I cannot hold on to it. It is fleeting. It has no explicit breadth. It explicitly has no breadth, no depth, no dimension whatsoever. If it did, I would be able to go into the past or the future, but I can't. I must live only in this current instant. The past is in my memory, and the future in my imagination. The present moment really is a zero. It has the deception of measurement, but it has no measurement at all.

A line is defined as a string of points. A point has no dimension. It takes up no space. It is the equivalent of a zero. It has only an address, if you will. A line has only its length, or two addresses, as it stretches between the two end-points and is an infinite string of points. It has no height or width. We can experience an entire line at once by placing it on a page. We see its length.

Time is an infinite series of moments. It is a line defined by length only, with many moments that have no true dimension. Experiencing time is like passing through the line point by point. We are stuck on the time line at a singular point. We cannot experience the future, an expectation of more present moments, until it becomes the present.

As all moments are points, represented as zero, these are all just an infinite number of zeroes. A hundred thousand zeroes is still just a zero. There is not one element of time that has any dimension. Life is Maya, a perfect illusion.

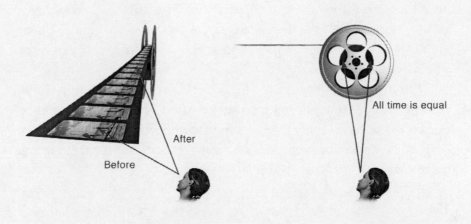

Before   After   All time is equal

Turn the film canister sideways, and the entire story exists in a single plane, in the single moment that you are in. Time is simply one perspective, one angle of interpretation.

Past   **Present**   **Future**

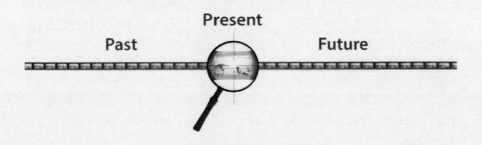

The Present is a Point just passed.
—David Russell

For God, time is both non-existent and infinite (since these two concepts are basically the same thing.) If I told you there was a penny across the room, but you could only get to it by taking trips half as long as the distance remaining between you and the penny, how long would it take you to reach it? The answer is you never would, because half the distance is never the whole distance. There are an infinite number of halves to reach your goal, and therefore you will never reach it.

Let me put it another way. The Earth circles the sun in a single year of four seasons. If you are outside the Earth, what difference does it make how long it takes us to circle the sun? Better yet, how long does it take for Neptune to circle the sun? Who cares? It has no relevance to us here on Earth.

Your version of time has no relevance to God. He is outside your plane of existence.

Man uses time as a way to define his perceptions, his experiences. But time does not actually exist outside of this world. They say goldfish have a three second memory. To goldfish, time exists only as a short line.

When you have a nightmare, you experience feelings. You might be upset or see things that terrify you or make you sad. Is it real? When you wake from the dream, you feel comforted because then you know it was not real, but you are sweating and your heart is pumping because when you were dreaming your entire body was convinced it was real. It was real for you, before you awoke and entered a different reality. You felt the emotions and your blood was racing. Only once you woke could you understand it was "just a dream."

> *Tomorrow hopes we've learned something from yesterday.*
> *—John Wayne*

If you go to the movies and watch John Wayne on the screen, you will fall for the deception of a "moving picture," even though the movie is just a collection of still images. They are only motionless pictures, but shown in a way as to make you believe there is movement on the screen. You watch as The Duke shoots and talks and rides, but Wayne died many years ago. This is effective deception. You become emotionally invested in the film. You are worried about the hero, and whether the heroine will live or die. Your heart races and your mouth goes dry. You physically fall for it although you mentally know it is all trickery because John Wayne is dead and buried and you rented a DVD. If you went up to the screen to get some of John Wayne's DNA or any physical evidence that he was there, good luck, because he was never actually on the screen.

Because time has no dimension, we are, like John Wayne in the film, in a series of snapshots called moments, that are strung together to give us the illusion of continuity, an imagined feature. There is no movement in the film, or in our "time."

Showing now, at a life of your choosing.

If you ever want to know anything about this life, you will not find it in this life. This life is the projection on the screen. Our souls are quasi film producers.

Good vibrations.

In their research, nuclear scientists and physicists traveled into the smallness of matter. What they discovered as they delved further into its physical make up, is that matter is more space than substance. Objects can be broken down into elements such as atoms: protons, neutrons and electrons. These small particles were very interesting because, although the size of the atom is large, in comparison, its density—the amount of matter inside the atom—is relatively small. (More space than substance.) Picture cream, and then whipping it. Atoms are like whipped cream—more air than substance. Quantum physicists put the final cap on the research when they proved that the smallest element of matter, the quark, is only energy. Vibrations. And the quark is the building block of all physical substance. What seems like matter, what seems firm, really is just energy vibrating, *giving the appearance of being solid*. So matter is actually vibrating energy.

Matter is energy.

Physical matter is actually energy, or spirit. By extrapolation, physical laws can be applied equally on the spiritual plane. The physical and metaphysical laws that we have discussed rule spiritually. This is why your decisions (spiritual) have effect on the physical plane. They have actual consequences that cannot be avoided. Cause and Effect, Balance; they all apply on the spiritual plane as well as the physical plane. There is no difference between the two because everything you experience as real is manifested spiritual energy.

> *What is mind? No matter.*
> *What is matter? Never mind.*
> *—Bishop Berkeley*

So do we live at all then?
Maya is the answer.

Chapter 4

Is This Life Real?

What shall be up shall be down—what shall be down shall be up.
—The Tibetan Book of the Dead

The short answer to the question this chapter tackles is "NO." That begs for an explanation, so here goes.

We 'live' on Earth like we experience our dreams in life. Dreams are beautifully analogous. There cannot be two realities. There cannot be a reality on earth, and also a reality with God who is forever. One must be a deception. If God really exists, then this world cannot be the true reality. The simple fact is that from our point of view, we will never be able to judge the whole. We are inside of it, and therefore cannot view it properly. We reside in the celluloid; the canister encloses us.

Take a picture; it lasts longer.

God creates us in His image—but God does not end, nor does He get sick—so this reference is to our eternal souls, not to our finite bodies.

True to the law of polarity, if this life is not permanent and only ephemeral and fleeting, then there must be truth and reality on the other side. The only separation between the two is death and birth. Simplistically, we are the negative; and the actual photograph is where we exist without the pretext of time and matter, after we die.

Welcome to "Opposite World."

This life is in direct polarity to that one, and here everything changes constantly. That is how we are assured that heaven is unvarying. When you started reading this chapter a few minutes ago, life was different. Already in the past few moments, continents have shifted, people have died, babies were born, married, divorced, and injured. People have lied, loved, made a deal, lost a deal. Life is different than it was only a few moments ago. It is like taking a bubble bath, where what appears to be mountains of foam changes slowly into just some bubbles that pop and move. In this life there is no permanence. (As they say, only two things are certain: death and taxes!) In the afterlife, the real life, everything is permanent. It is the opposite of this life.

> *If you understand, things are just as they are;*
> *If you do not understand, things are just as they are.*
> *—Zen proverb*

Scientists understand now that matter only exists in our perception. Matter is actually energy. It is not immovable. It is constantly shifting, so quickly we cannot perceive it with our natural human senses. But some changes we can observe. We are born and we grow, transforming constantly: our hairstyle, our friends, our furniture, our shoes. If you take an 87-year-old man and hold his baby photo next to him, you would not be able to tell if it was the same person; we change so much throughout our lives.

What is the single constant in a man's life? His soul.

You are born. You grow up and get older and older until your body no longer resembles your younger self at all. You get frail and then you die. And in that moment you are completely lost, everything is taken from you: your life, your family, your friends and all your worldly possessions. In that moment of your greatest desperation, you are truly born. In that death, you are reunited with your friends and loved ones again in eternity, and your feeling of loss is replaced with an absolute feeling of loving that never fades. That is why it is called heaven. It is a feeling of fulfillment and richness and of course it has to do with your personal relationships. Heaven is not a place where you sit around with God and chew the fat, just the two of you. It is a place overflowing with all the souls you have loved and who love you, in communion with God.

Is the human soul subject to the laws of space and time?

Human beings are required to go through the book of life page after page, word by word, because we are bound to our illusions. Time and matter appear to us as we are supposed to experience them. In a film the characters seem like they are actually moving, although that is not the case. The film is a rapid series of still photos, projected with light onto a wall, which creates a perfect illusion for us to be immersed in the story. It meets and manipulates our emotions.

Permanence is illusion.

Time and matter are malleable materials, like unchained buoys more than anchors. They are also the parameters in which we experience life, and as such they seem very real to us. We experience this world as authentic because God stages it all for us. If the deception were any less, we might too easily see through it. Would saving a life have the same meaning, if you understood that it was not a real life? Of course not. It has to be 'real.' The consequences must be 'real' and so must the danger. Our sacrifices feel and seem authentic because we experience the joy or the pain inherent in them, as it was designed.

Our emotional attachment validates our physical experience.

Would you honestly let your children run out into the busy street to play with knives? Of course not. To protect them, you put them in a playpen, then in safeguarded rooms, then an elementary school with proper security. For his own security, you would not allow your toddler to run around a grocery store, but there is a pretend grocery store at his play group where he can make believe he is really shopping. To him, the plastic veggies and fake milk cartons are real.

God cares equally for His children here on earth.

So, what is real?

God—He is eternal. Your soul—made in His image. Love. And love transcends all, because it is linked more intricately to your soul than to your physicality. We come into this life to change our souls so they can come incrementally closer to God. And that is as it should be, for here is where the work is done. You are inundated every day with decisions designed to impact your soul. In essence, these choices are binary, meaning they are either/or. They will all come down to the basic question: Will you be for or against God? Supporting life or against life? Building up or tearing down? Furthering your soul or holding it back? Toward goodness or headed for evil?

Right or wrong?

As you make these decisions you create the clay that molds your soul. That is why God warns us not to speak or think bad things. Everything starts in the mind, and thinking evil things gives them a birth or foothold. When we put attention, structure and action to maliciousness, we create ugliness in our souls. Since it is a spiritual decision first and foremost, it is best to think, speak and do no evil.

Your soul becomes more complete and more beautiful, the more virtuous your decisions and the more your character is shaped by facing life's challenges. Your body is still simply the clay that forms the bronze. The clay plays a critical role in molding the bronze, but once the metal has cooled, you can knock the clay right off and it crumbles to the floor. The clay form, your body, has lost its purpose. The body has a beginning and an end, while just the opposite is true of the spirit.

What is more real, the clay mold or the bronze sculpture?

Life is an ongoing process of awakening. On this earth, evil is everywhere, temptation is relentless, and your soul is continually at risk. Step by step, moment by moment, you move forward and craft the depths of your soul to mirror the perfection of God. It is an awakening, a long and difficult process, but eventually you will get there.

Life is a school for our souls.

When you see children in a school, you know one thing for certain: they are there to learn. They are not doctors or lawyers, or they would not be in school. The very fact that they are in school tells you they are students. They still have lessons to learn. A doctor does not graduate med school and then start over again—what would be the point?

The same is true of our souls. That we are on this earth means we are still students. The current Pope, you and I, we are all still earthbound spirits in school. Some of us are closer to graduation than others, but we cannot deny why we are here. And if we come back again and again, we may find that we see the same souls again and again, as we are on similar journeys. Just like in school, when you leave second grade, have summer vacation, and then go back for third grade, you are likely to see most of the same students again in your classroom. We meet the same souls over and over again in death and in life, because we are on similar paths. They are our companions on the journey to God.

$3 + x = 10$ *solve for* x.

Just as the problems in school are planned for the use of the students, and then they are erased, our life-problems are for our personal growth, and cease to exist once solved. After the blackboard is cleaned, and the next class, one year younger, enters, the same problems go back up on the board. They are recycled for the next students. In life, we are never in completely unique situations. All these problems have come before, and will be explored again. In a way, you might say they cannot be solved because their purpose is to educate and inform, and to that end the solutions are truly a part of each problem.

The challenges we face, together with their solutions, are part of this world, and therefore part of the great illusion of life. They disappear when they are no longer necessary, but they prepare us for the next step, and that is the afterlife. Time and matter do not have the eternal properties that we naturally ascribe to them. It makes no difference how strong we would build a castle or how impenetrable the granite and the steel; eventually nothing will be left of it. The moment we build it, it wants to disintegrate. Everything that humans create is in a state of decay. It all wants to return to dust, to entropy.

Even a plant that grows from a seed is intended to decay and return to the earth. The great sequoia trees that grow so tall and wide have their lives for a limited amount of time. The life span of a sequoia may appear like a very long time to us, but our narrow perspective distorts our perception. Those majestic trees may seem timeless to a small human dwarfed by their size and age, but once the life force has lapsed, they return to mulch, like the rest of us. From God's point of view, your life on earth is a castle built of sand. He understands the tides of time that you barely perceive, because he created the oceans.

Eternity is not infinite time, but the absence of time.

Compared to an eternity, 50 or 60 years is not even the blink of an eye. Now, try to adjust mentally to living on an eternal plane.

You can get back to me on that ...

Reality is outside of this world, and therefore unfettered by time, unlimited by the deception of matter. Reality is always. It is the opposite of anything finite. The process of discovering this certainty is like a considered, unmistakable awakening.

In this life we age, but our souls never age. Souls are not shackled to time. Think about your soul for a moment. Does it feel old? No, it just feels like a soul.

You believe that time is passing by.
You are wrong.
Time stands still. You are passing.

Pinch your arm. It seems so much like you. You think that is you, but it is not you. It is pork chops and beef stew from last month, a few salads and some chocolate bars. You are what you eat? Physically, yes, but spiritually, not quite. Spiritually, you are what you *think*. You are what you *do*. You can feel when you touch your arm, because you are supposed to. It is part of the illusion of life, but that does not make it real any more than seeing a movie proves that John Wayne shot a man.

> *Man is what he believes.*
> *—Chekhov*

Think about yourself being conceived. You changed from two cells to four to eight cells, to a fetus and then a child. Eventually, you became an adult human being. You did all this growth and transformation by eating and drinking. By consuming food, you altered all those strange particles into what you call "yourself" today. But it is not you. It is rented atoms. Many of your body's cells wear out and are replaced. Even solid things like bone are actually living and growing, changing and exchanging tissue. Medical science has determined with certainty how long it takes for blood to regenerate, for instance. According to recent research, in fact, it seems that on average your body cells are less than 16 years old! Yet our appearance betrays that truth. The physique of a 90-year-old woman is hardly anything like her 16-year-old self, not to mention comparing her to what she looked like at birth. We are like ghosts wandering through this life from one moment to the next, in which 80 years seems long but is just a blink. The reality lies only in the souls we pilot.

You only hurt the ones you love.

You cannot hurt a soul, unless it is your own. By doing immoral or bad things, you alter your soul in a negative way. When you eat pork chops and chocolate they eventually become your flesh. Your thoughts and actions become your soul. If someone does something nice for you, it is easy to smile and be nice back, and that is good for the shape of your soul. But if evil attacks you, and you respond in kind, your soul is affected as well. This is the way God designed it, so we might make choices and shape our souls with our own free will. The illusion of reality on this plane is perfect; we are affected and concerned for others and encouraged to act accordingly.

Every person that comes before you is an opportunity …
for you.
—Pope Benedict

This world is all imaginary, though it seems very real to us. But think about it for a minute. Say you are having a bad day. You hate your job, you burned the toast, and your clunker of a car is going to cost several hundred dollars for a tune up. You feel like the weight of the world is on your shoulders. Then, when you get to work, your best friend from college calls to say he is coming to town and wants to take you to the ball game that night. All of a sudden, the weight is lifted from your shoulders and you are happy. How did that happen? You still have the same job and the same car, and the toast is still in the trash, but you have a lilt in your step and a smile on your face. It is literally like you were just looking in one direction, at the darkness, and then something made you turn your face, and a beautiful light shown upon you. You are experiencing the exact same circumstances in a completely different way. That is proof that it is all imaginary.

Change your perspective; change your life.

Before, you had the illusion that life was awful and depressing, but life is an illusion that can easily be modified. One quick phone call convinced you that life is yet exciting and hopeful. And what is a phone call? A reproduction of a voice you recognize—it is not even the real voice. We are so conditioned to accept this chimera of life that we find it very difficult to escape in order to view it from a different perspective. Like your screensaver on the computer, you are the one who can change it. No one else has the code to switch the picture, and the photo is just several thousands of pixels, but when it comes on the screen it makes you smile. It is an illusion, but it affects you. And if you have the code, you can exchange that photo for another one at any time, because it is your illusion alone. That is your life, too.

I am an optimist.
It does not seem too much use being anything else.
—Winston Churchill

When the bad guy in the film dies, is he really dead? No. He is an actor, and they paint blood on him, and they all pretend that he is dead, and perhaps we are relieved that the bad guy is gone out of the film because we are emotionally invested. Your emotions are in direct correlation with what you see, but in truth you see nothing but lights and shadows playing tricks. The bad guy did not die; in fact he was not even there! All of it was an illusion, meant to fool you into believing. Now, with computer graphics, we can generate fully realistic imagery from binary code. Ones and zeros. It is beyond my poor comprehension to understand how a series of one and zeros can make and color a picture that is extraordinarily realistic, but it happens every day now. As we become more adept at the trickery of computer generated graphics, depicting more realistic scenes, the evidence for the illusory quality of this life grows. We can be Tiger Woods on the TV screen, hitting a winning shot on the 18th at Pebble Beach, and the screen will even show the sweat on his brow (our brow). Delving deeper into virtual reality is, in turn, a great correlation to the experience our souls have in this "real" version of life. How much longer will the ever-fuzzier line between virtual and real exist? How long will it take us to recognize the metaphor that virtual reality is to our own real lives, as our real lives is the metaphor for eternal life? Sorry, I didn't mean to get too "out there" for you, but the parallels need to be acknowledged. We are entirely seduced by our movie culture, the creation of illusions. It is no surprise we find it challenging to believe that this life we are living is, in itself, one grand trick. But it is.

There is no death because there is no life.

That does not mean that if you do a bad thing that bad thing does not exist, because every thought and each action in this life transfers onto our souls. The idea that life is illusory simply points to how authentic God must be, in contrast, according to the Law of Polarity. God appears fictitious to us, but we are the ones who are unreal. We are in this great play, where we are free to act without really harming anyone else. The only person you can genuinely affect is your own soul. Once you truly absorb these concepts, you can perceive the amazing grace of God, and grasp the notions of good and evil and understand them in an entirely different light.

> *Good for the body is the work of the body,*
> *good for the soul the work of the soul,*
> *and good for either the work of the other.*
> *—Henry David Thoreau*

Imagine that you have died, and now you are on the outside of this world, observing. You are in a state of enlightenment, watching and witnessing that this world is a school for souls where no real harm can be done, no true permanent physical harm. It is like watching your own children playing in the schoolyard. They pretend-drive toy cars, playing traffic, but nothing can really happen to them. What happens to the toys is not nearly as important as how the children behave towards each other. If there is a crash, nobody really gets hurt, but you can see that the one boy did want to hurt the other little boy. His *intent* was the crucial element, because his character shapes his soul.

You should not kill, but if you do, the killing is not the critical feature, because death is not more than illusion. The significant component is your *intention* to kill. If you kill physically, that is disruptive on the *mortal* level, but it has smaller importance when compared with your intent to do harm on the *moral* level, which has a direct impact on your soul.

You cannot be deeply asleep and totally awake at the same time. It is either one or the other. Since this world is an imposter, reality is where our souls go after we die here. When we pass into the next life, we reach a state of consciousness as a soul and realize, again, how safe we actually were in that lifetime. One thing that is repeated and repeated in the Bible is that we should not fear, but follow God. This life is just our human dream, but our souls are still safe in their "beds," as we dream this fleeting life. So relax, fear not, but do not forget your purpose here on earth: to face life, make moral decisions and see them through to their natural conclusions, to your fullest potential, all the while never losing sight of God.

We do not see things as they are; we see things as we are.
—Talmud

Your team loses the soccer game 3-2. You are sad for the rest of the afternoon, but does it really matter the following day? The weights you lift in the gym, are they "real," meaning do they have relevance in your life outside the gym? No. Remember the test you scored well on in seventh grade? No. It's gone. It never really was, in fact. Life is not real, because life is the dream-state for your 'death,' and your death-state is truly real. What you envision as your end, your death, is actually your homecoming into life: your soul's permanent communion with God.

And in the end, it's not the years in your life that count.
It's the life in your years.
—Abraham Lincoln

Chapter 5

What Is a Soul?

Tis true my form is something odd,
But blaming me is blaming God.
Could I create myself anew,
I would not fail in pleasing you.
If I could reach from pole to pole,
Or grasp the ocean with a span,
I would be measured by the soul,
The mind's the standard of the man.
—Isaac Watts

What isn't, is. What is, never actually was.

What appears is not really the way it is. As you get into the smallest known particles in quantum physics, you access the building blocks of everything, quarks. Quarks are only energy. We experience matter as solid, but that is only our perception. On the smallest scale, fundamentally, matter is energy within emptiness.

So, then, what is energy?

Everything. And your soul is also a real, substantial part of that. As tangible as lava, in a sense. You cannot touch lava, as it would destroy you. You cannot touch your soul because that would destroy this illusion of life. You cannot hear a dog whistle, either, because you are not a dog. You may not perceive your soul, but it is apparent to others.

> *Care I for the limb, the thews, the stature, bulk,*
> *and big assemblance of a man! Give me the spirit.*
> *—William Shakespeare*

Your soul is not your conscience. Your soul is the energy or force that bridges both life and death. The plain truth is that your physical appearance is not you at all, but it resembles you for the purpose of this life. Your soul resides in your physical body like you ride in a car: it gets you to a final destination. Through the use of your corporal body the soul has the opportunity for growth and transformation to become closer to God.

You are not what you eat.

What you touch and feel when you put your hand on your arm, and flesh meets flesh, was chocolate pudding, hamburgers and sushi only three weeks ago. But that is not *you.*

> *The virtues we acquire, which develop slowly within us, are*
> *the invisible links that bind each one of our existences to*
> *the others—existences which the spirit alone remembers, for*
> *Matter has no memory for spiritual things.*
> *—Honoré de Balzac*

Picture a young boy, playing with blocks. He builds an intricate castle, and then is called to dinner. What does he do when his fantasy life inside the castle walls is extinguished? He joyfully kicks the blocks over like the playthings they are, and the castle crumbles to the floor.

Your body is constantly sloughing off dead skin cells. You brush your hair and discard the hair that stays on the brush. You throw away what is no longer useful to you, although it was once part of you. It still contains your DNA but that is a technicality. Do you miss it? The same applies to our gross anatomy: the corpse that we each will leave behind still contains our basic physical shape and our DNA but that is all there is to it. The soul discards the body just like you blow your nose. The body is really only particles that have been put together like building blocks to give you your earthly shape. They are a collection that you borrow for a short time to allow you to walk this earth and fully indulge in the physical part of the human experience: eating, drinking, loving, sorrow, sensations like heat, cold and pain, and so on. These are all things that would not be possible for you without a body. These particles that make up your body change constantly and rapidly. From newborn infant all the way to dying human, and then to ashes and dust, you shed this body after you have ceased needing it.

The body is fleeting. The soul endures.

The body is but the temporary host for your soul. What clearly is you is the force behind you, the force that drives you. That force is eternal. It is not matter. It does not change from chocolate pudding, passing through the digestive track to become part of a finger or a tooth. You cannot lose it and the only way you can change its shape, throughout eternity, is by thoughts, decisions and actions here in life. The choices that you make, no matter how insignificant you believe them to be, have great relevance to what happens to your soul's shape.

What is soul? It's like electricity—we don't really know what it is,
but it's a force that can light a room.
—Ray Charles

Arnold Schwarzenegger's body speaks to us. It announces that long ago he decided to put an enormous amount of time and effort into building a strong and muscular physique. What we recognize is the end effect of this decision: well-developed and toned muscles that resulted from facing resistance over and over again. If he had done the opposite, and just lazed about on the beach doing nothing, he would certainly look different. There would stand a flabby man with loose flesh and very little muscle mass. Had he decided to eat a lot of junk food and combined it with lack of exercise, then he would also be very overweight by now, perhaps enough that he would have trouble walking. Clearly, he chose the gym—more than the average man or woman. He created the Schwarzenegger body that became a kind of beauty ideal in our society, and that physique, combined with other attributes, gained him fame, fortune and vast success.

What do we all desire? We all want to be beautiful like Charlize Theron or handsome like Brad Pitt. We want to be strong and healthy like Roger Federer, and we want to be young and un-creased. That is a common western beauty ideal we can all relate to. In other societies, the ideal may be for women to be more rounded about the hips while men may wish for a particularly impressive beard growth. All societies commonly have a fundamental beauty ideal that is generally recognized by the members of that culture and that ideal is passionately emulated.

Conversely, people who are greatly divergent from the accepted ideal are often rejected by society, which may be shocked, saddened or disgusted. Joseph Merrick, the unfortunate Elephant Man, was shamed and mocked and denigrated. The opening poem of this chapter was especially important to him, for obvious reasons. He was rejected as a twelve-year-old by his own family, and as a young teen earned his living as a participant in a freak show. Members of the British society all agreed on one thing: they did not want to look like Merrick. His ungainly appearance was entirely undesirable, because society's beauty ideal seduces us to the exclusion of deeper pursuits. Beauty relates first and foremost to what the eye can see, so we go to the gym in order to sculpt our bodies. We buy attractive clothes. We go to beauty salons, and undergo facial treatments, liposuction, breast enhancements. For men, it has now become fashionable to have chest implants or to wax off their body hair. There is a plethora of television shows dedicated to showcasing makeovers and plastic surgery. People spend an incredible amount of time and money and energy enhancing their appearance on a strictly superficial level, and society as a whole rewards them for it. This is an unfortunate travesty.

> *Since love grows within you, so beauty grows.*
> *For love is the beauty of the soul.*
> *—Saint Augustine*

One of the most important works of fiction about the human condition and the relationship between soul and person is <u>The Picture of Dorian Gray</u>, by Oscar Wilde. In the story, a painted portrait of Dorian represents his soul. Dorian behaves despicably, exhibiting greed, selfishness and other moral evils. His ugly behavior manifests only on the painting, and not on the person demonstrating it. In fact, Dorian does not even age. The portrait of the attractive young man slowly ages in a horrifically grotesque way, while outwardly the person of Dorian remains as attractive as ever.

As a metaphor, the story serves us very well. Your soul is the portrait of your thoughts and deeds. It is the imprint you make on others, like a footprint in sand. Although the foot is gone, its effect remains. Your soul is a collection of all the impressions your actions have made.

The human soul has still greater need of the ideal than of the real.
It is by the real that we exist; it is by the ideal that we live.
—Victor Hugo

The Bible holds up angels as being very close to God. Angels are presented for us to emulate, and they are unassailably nearly as perfect and as beautiful as God Himself. They are never described as plain, mousy looking, or average. The words used to describe them are always flattering superlatives, along the lines of "beautiful," "tall," "strong," and "magnificent." They are kind, loving and protective. There are no angels with bad teeth or foul breath. There is never any mention of an ugly angel or an angel with dirty clothing. But do not confuse their apparent beauty with physicality, of which they have none. The splendor they possess is modeled to us in a physical sense because that is the only way we can appreciate it. Angelic beauty is reflective of soul beauty, not the mere earthly superficial good looks our society is addicted to.

Living is being born slowly. It would be a little too easy
if we could borrow ready-made souls.
—Antoine de Saint-Exupéry

Your *intentions* and your *actions* create your soul. No beauty salon or fancy clothes can touch that. You not only live *with* your decisions but you *become* your decisions. Your soul has seen God as the most ideal entity and the most beautiful, and it has determined to become like God. We all endeavor to become like what we most admire, so God is your soul's beauty ideal. God is perfection, love, grace and forgiveness. Those qualities are what will most beautify and gratify your soul, in its pursuit of God. The only way to accomplish soul improvement is by living a life here on earth, and that experience must be dominated by good and wise decisions, by godly virtues in your living.

The most basic test of this life is to develop our souls in God's image.

In order to develop a soul that is attractive to God we have to face resistance. We do so by choosing to enter this world, just like Schwarzenegger went to the gym. By facing the problems of this world we are modifying the appearance of our souls. Imagine you can look at your soul, which is not touched by time and not subject to the constraints of matter. Now imagine that every lie, every deception, every time you stabbed someone in the back, cheated someone of what was rightly theirs, took something from someone else that did not belong to you is etched into your soul. And, I am not just talking about one lifetime, I am talking about all the bad actions of all the lifetimes you have ever had. These things are all present in your soul. All the traces of all these bad actions and thoughts cannot be changed once you separate from your earthly body, just like the painting is changed in Dorian Gray's attic.

Ordinary riches can be stolen, real riches cannot.
In your soul are infinitely precious things that cannot be taken from you.
—Oscar Wilde

After you die and leave your physical body behind you are simply your soul, which is, as always, completely visible to God. There is no cloth to hide behind, no Armani suit or dental veneers. There is no way to change the appearance of your soul either, though you may desire it. The only way to change the constitution of the soul is to face the resistance of this world again and again. All the small challenges change your soul in similarly small increments. Bodybuilding requires more than just one visit to the gym, and souls do not change completely over one lifetime. Meet the challenges of this life and you are creating a different soul by doing so. Better your soul through being more truthful, selfless and loving. You can tell the kind of people who truly make use of this life to advance their souls. They are the ones who always seem to have a good word for everyone and who are quick to help when someone is in a bind. When given the chance to join in disparaging someone, they keep their mouths shut and even come to that person's defense. Everyone wants to be around them because their company always feels good. They are not, however, the kind of people who have never had problems in their lives. You may find these people in cancer wards of large hospitals, in prisons or in poor neighborhoods. They are people who have faced hardship. The same way that Arnold used the gym equipment, whatever adversities they tackled became the tools for them to improve their souls.

*It **is** the thought that counts, after all.*

Too few people know the inspiring story of the R in the H&R Block®. In his later years, Richard Bloch, one of the founders of the large accounting firm, was diagnosed with terminal lung cancer, and his doctors told him he had three months to live. Of course, Bloch could have taken issue with God. He had been a faithful, churchgoing Christian all his life. Why would God allow him to get (or give him) lung cancer, a particularly difficult and painful death? Bloch could have turned away from God, embittered and disappointed, and many of us would not have blamed him one iota. But Bloch did quite the opposite. Rather than condemning God and the unfairness of life in general, he decided to view his disease as an opportunity for personal growth. He turned his energies toward helping as many other people as possible and so he put his considerable financial resources into finding out more about the illness. He also prayed to God. He prayed that he would accept God's will, whatever it was, and asked that he be allowed to survive so that he could continue to help others with the disease. He survived both lung cancer and later colon cancer, and died 26 years after his first diagnosis. He wrote three books about battling and surviving cancer. Today, anyone afflicted with cancer can benefit from the R.A. Bloch Cancer Foundation hotline, which matches the newly diagnosed cancer patient to someone who has recovered from the same disease.

It could not have been a simple decision on his part to manage his illness in this way. That is part of the test of character. I am certain that he had many differing emotions concerning his sickness and God's will in his treatment, but through his faith and belief, he most assuredly changed the image of his soul with this ordeal.

Just like the body builder who looks in the mirror and sees that his stomach looks good but his arms still need improvement, we can also choose our "problem areas" and exercise them. When we look into our inner-mirrors we cannot help but see that we really are not ready yet for the Kingdom of Heaven. We are not 'dressed' to enter a place that is perfect. We need more work. It takes many trips to the gym to perfect the body, and it takes many visits to this life, many lifetimes, to perfect the soul. Some people have a faster path and some people's paths will be considerably slower. Some people are hopelessly frustrated by life. They react to the problems in their lives with aggression or even violence. But even those people will make some progress. Or they may, in the eleventh hour, make enormous progress.

> *The soul is placed in the body like a rough diamond,*
> *and must be polished, or the luster of it will never appear.*
> *—Daniel Defoe*

Karla Faye Tucker was a woman who was executed in Texas in 1998. She was the kind of person you might think was beyond redemption and soul growth. After a turbulent life of prostitution and drugs she murdered a woman named Deborah Thornton with an axe and was sent to death row. During her trial, she read the Bible and accepted Jesus. She became a Christian. She remained on death row for nearly 14 years and was even responsible for converting her victim's brother, Ronald Carlson, who visited her there, and who opposed the death penalty. People who witnessed her religious transformation will not easily forget the last few years of Tucker's life as she tried to lead other death row prisoners on the path to God. Some of her last words were,

I love all of you very much. I am going to be face to face with Jesus now. Warden Baggett, thank all of you so much.
You have been so good to me. I love all of you very much.
I will see you all when you get there.
I will wait for you.
—Karla Faye Tucker

Prison officials choked back tears as they announced the completion of her execution. What touched everyone, most likely, was how she used the resistance she faced, which was insurmountable, as a means to grow not only her own soul but also to try to help advance the soul growth of those around her. She seems to have proved that it is never too late to seek God and to ask him to find you. Everyone evolves. Every soul strives to a higher ideal. It desires to do so, being hungry to make its way toward the light.

The shape of your soul has only one determining factor: **free choice**, which is the greatest gift God bestowed on mankind. Your soul looks exactly the way you behave. There is very little connection between your physical appearance in this life and your soul. We all know people who are physically stunning but sorely lacking in inner beauty.

Your soul thrives on your righteous thoughts and actions.

Offering a kind word, or a smile, or giving a generous hand to someone in need obviously will reflect positively on your soul. Sometimes it is easier; other times, harder. Is that unfair? Does that mean that we are not given equal opportunity to show kindness and hence advance our soul growth? Some people in the gym are working out with twenty pounds and others bench press one-eighty. Some have just started and others have been lifting for several years. They are all in different stages of their total exercise plan. Whatever situation you are in, you have been placed there to advance your soul.

God does not throw dice.

Regardless of your ability, or lack thereof, to understand the lessons of this life, you are exactly where you are meant to be in any given moment. Everything is as it should be. Questioning your challenges equates to second-guessing God or disputing free will, and that is no different from a student in school who wonders why his teacher has not yet put him, at age seven, into twelfth grade. Children attend school to solve problems and after they have successfully worked out a certain number of those, they move up to the next grade where more challenges await them, until in the end they have mastered the highest grade and are allowed to graduate. They are on the road to graduation as in life we are on the road to salvation.

By behaving righteously, despite your challenges, you elevate yourself, but if you run from your problems then you are distancing yourself from the very opportunities you require! Your soul needs growth and cultivation, like a flower needs water and sunshine to blossom. See that there is an entire plant and not just a leaf, and sometimes the rain is a good thing. Your problems force you to grow and gain strength, so that your soul will be more perfect each day. It is up to you to capitalize on your trials, rather than waste time complaining or longing for altered situations that are not within reach, for stations not on your intended road.

The Body doesn't have a Soul; the Soul has a Body.

Chapter 6

What is Death and Why Must We Die?

Why should we be startled by death?
Life is a constant putting off of the mortal coil—
coat, cuticle, flesh and bones, all old clothes.
—Henry David Thoreau

My father was in his seventies when he died a few years ago. He was a vital, fit, and active man, but he suffered a heart attack while napping on the couch, and never woke again.

Three weeks after my father passed away, he appeared to me in a dream. In my dream, my brother and I were in my parents' bed, sobbing because of our loss. I was perhaps five, wearing pajamas that I have long since forgotten, but I recognized them in the dream. My father was in his thirties in appearance, very handsome and charming, as I knew he had been in his prime, but even better looking, glorious. He smiled, trying to comfort my brother and me as we cried over his death. He said, amiably, "Do not cry. If you knew where I am right now, you wouldn't cry. You would laugh. You would rejoice. You would not shed one tear.

"If anybody should cry, it is I. You still have your lives to live, but that is the way it is supposed to be. I am where I should be, in a place more beautiful than you could ever imagine."

This life is the dream from which death wakes us.

Death is the natural consequence of life, according to the Law of Cycles. It is our homecoming to God. The most beautiful day of our lives is our death day, in fact. Death is simply returning to God. As we pass from one year to the next, rather than mourning the past year, we celebrate the New Year, the moment of transition, distinguishing the old from the new. Death is also such a transition.

> *I know I am deathless.*
> *No doubt I have died myself ten thousand times before.*
> *I laugh at what you call dissolution,*
> *and I know the amplitude of time.*
> *—Walt Whitman*

We have a consistent renewal each day, at midnight. The cycle starts again, another twenty-four hours, another day, week, year. Spring transforms into summer, each and every year. Spring does not miss one year, or ever substitute for winter. Death is simply a marking point of our shift into another lifetime.

Death is a renewal.

This life is like a classroom. Imagine you are a first-grader. You and your class all go through similar tests throughout the year. You are joined by common experiences. Then it is summer vacation and you all part ways, only to reunite in the fall when school starts again. Some have grown, some less, but basically you are still all on the same path. After second grade comes third. Summer vacation falls in between, when you may not see your friends as much. For some, the separation is difficult, but when all the students see each other again in the fall, friendships and bonds pick up right where they left off. Vacation meant not seeing each other, but in the reunification the same relationships endure, although possibly somewhat changed. You may have made some enduring friendships, the close bonds that follow you throughout your school years, and even longer.

> *As we live through thousands of dreams in our present life,*
> *so is our present life only one of many thousands of such lives*
> *which we enter from the other more real life and then return*
> *after death. Our life is but one of the dreams of that more*
> *real life, and so it is endlessly, until the very last one, the very*
> *real, the life of God.*
> *—Count Leo Tolstoy*

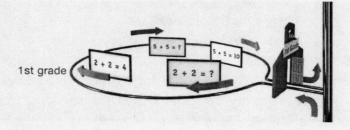

We are not all here as first-graders. We have close friends and family, souls that are very close to us, some of whom are closer to graduating than others. The good news is that we cannot lose them because when we are in heaven, nothing is lost. They might be out of sight, like over summer vacation, but they are there, waiting to find us again at the start of school next fall. Just as, on her doorstep, your mother would wrap you in her arms when you would come home for a visit, your loved ones await you at the gates of heaven, to welcome you home after death separated them from you. The only difference is that in heaven, joy is eternal. It does not wear off because in heaven you cannot lose your life; you cannot lose your love or your health or anything. Heaven is permanence. Heaven's eternity does not mean endless time. It means the absence of time.

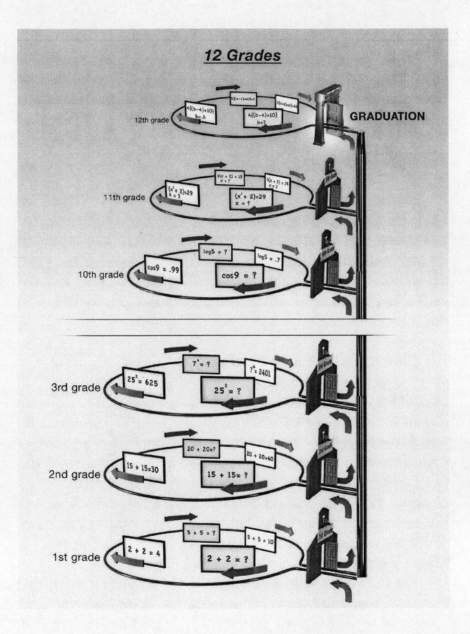

If there is no struggle there is no progress.
—Frederick Douglas

If you are in second grade, you must leave it to attend third grade. There is no third grade learning to be had in second grade. Once you are elevated in your abilities enough for third grade, you must move out of second.

The end justifies the means.

The hard thing about school is the learning, it is not the summers spent lounging at the beach or splashing on the lake. We understand that school is a difficult process that is necessary. If we truly understood what awaits us in death, we would leave this life without a care, with the understanding that the final end, the graduation, validates our struggles and the hardships we endure in this life.

Growing up in Austria I had a nanny named Pepi. She was a simple country girl, who got a job with our family and stayed with us until her death. She was not well educated and, in fact, I am not certain she ever really learned to read, but she was a woman who was absolutely full of love, and we all loved her back. She was also a person who could not lie. When she was 81, she got very sick and was hospitalized. She was still very full of life and determined to recover. I visited her in the hospital and she clung to my arm with fear and trepidation and said, "Marius, I don't want to die. Will I die? What will happen to me?" I tried my best to comfort her, but when I had to go I could see she was still very anxious.

The next day I visited her again. I immediately noticed that her mood, tone and even her appearance had completely changed. With a glow in her eyes that seemed other-worldly, she said, "Marius, I was there." "Where?" I asked. She said, "I was there, on the other side." She then proceeded to relate to me a near-death experience. I already knew that overnight the doctors had performed emergency procedures to resuscitate her. She said she had gone through a tunnel, passing over into a different realm where there was an amazing light and overwhelming love and instant knowledge. This was, of course, similar to many recorded near-death experiences. Because I knew her so well, I can assure you she had never heard of those accounts from other people. At the time, Küebler-Ross's work was the most current on near-death experiences, but Pepi had never heard of her. Regardless, the proof of her experience is her complete transformation. After they revived her, Pepi was no longer afraid. She became a believer in death, or "life after death." She realized that she was loved and ready to leave here, to shed her human body, rid herself of pain and the struggles of this world and enter into a purely spiritual form together with God.

Pepi went through life with a deformity. She was a tiny, plain woman who could barely walk on her bowed legs, but behind her eyes was the glow of a saint. After her death, she also appeared to me in a dream, and she was beautiful. It is often more difficult to describe what you see in a dream than how it made you feel. When I saw Pepi in my dream, it was definitely her, but in ethereal beauty, because the impression I had from her was intense splendor, much like I knew her soul to be. For sure, there was a reason why Pepi had to go through this life with such apparent resistance (her deformity,) but it was only that, organized for her for this life. In eternity, Pepi's soul is a lot more beautiful than her physical appearance on earth.

The secret of life and death lies in your breath.
—Johann Wolfgang von Goethe

You breathe in. You breathe out. Everything in life is rhythm. Everything is movement. Everything is transformation. The cycles of life are the same as the cycles of death, because death is just a part of life. Just like the full moon is followed by the half moon, and the new moon, and then the full moon again, over and over again, birth is followed by aging and then death, and then birth again. Midnight goes into dawn and the new day, and death goes into birth and the new life.

Without complicit death, life would be endless and valueless.

Nature has direction and purpose, even if we humans are blind to it. Everything we do in life has an effect in the amazing rhythm of life and those consequences are born out in our souls. Our bodies will turn to dust and other more useful bits and pieces, but our souls that preceded them will go on, just like the idea of a building still lives in the mind of the architect, though the building may be destroyed by fire.

> *It is not more surprising to be born twice than once;*
> *everything in nature is resurrection.*
> *—Voltaire*

An architect conceives of a building—not just the foundation or the roof, but the entire building in all its glory. He does not envision an old building that is crumbling. When my father appeared to me in my dream, he did not arrive as an old run-down decrepit corpse. He came to me as he was in the prime of life, as he was in his soul. My father was a very handsome man, but in my dream he was infinitely more handsome because he was not bound to this earth any longer, and so there was a light quality about him that shown. The light of eternity sparkled through him.

> *Jesus said to her, 'I am the resurrection and the life.*
> *He who believes in Me, though he may die, he shall live.*
> *And whoever lives and believes in Me shall never die ..."*
> *(John 11:25-26)*

Many years ago I was sleeping on a beach in Nigeria and what I dreamt was so realistic that it has stayed with me for all these years. I dreamt that I died and awoke on the other side as a soul. Instantly, I was completely at peace. I immediately knew God; I felt His light, His warmth, His infinite love. Right away, I understood everything and I had knowledge of everything. I was saved, not lost, in my feeling. That experience stayed with me. Once I awoke and I got out of my sleeping bag, that feeling stayed with me for hours, and for several days more I experienced this total rescue of my soul. I was exuberant, full of life and hope. It was like walking on clouds. Since then I have had this dream several more times. It is that incredible feeling of being saved right after I thought I was abandoned that creates this wondrous sentiment of euphoria that is with me always, and feeds my faith.

Death is not an end, but a transition.

In all the studied religions of the world, death is never the end. Many religions made the practice of burying their dead with travel accessories for the journey. In Egypt, they would bury the king with his living consorts to accompany him (poor girls).

In his book, <u>90 Minutes in Heaven</u>, Don Piper, a pastor, recounts his true story. Piper was pronounced dead and remained so, crushed inside his own car for 90 minutes, until another pastor prayed and sang hymns over him, and ostensibly brought him back from heaven. It is a fascinating story, but the crucial point for Mr. Piper is that heaven was so wonderful, as he describes in the book, that he was furious with God for insisting he go back to earth to a life of ceaseless rehabilitation, great pain, and tremendous frustration. His body was badly damaged in the accident and his situation was one of terrific struggle. He had seen the other side, so what was the point of being alive? He wanted to be back there, where there was endless happiness and peace, not here on earth. He also realized that he was special, as being one who knew without doubt what awaited him upon his death. Eventually, through prayer and healing, he learned to rejoice in his newfound exceptionality, and to use it to help others. But he still battles with the temptation of heaven's pure joy and serenity. It is the most amazing love convergence that one could possibly imagine. What lies beyond is sweet and inviting, almost irresistible. Most of us do not have that impression of death. Piper points out that even his description does not do justice to the experience he had. But most of us probably do not have his discipline, either, and we would no longer be tied to earth by our own choice if we found out for certain what lay beyond the great sleep. At the least, that knowledge would certainly change the way we live our lives today. Luckily, life has purpose, and therefore God imbued all creatures with a will to live and a fear of death.

Death is to birth as the dawn is to dusk.

Death is the conversion point from a transformational life into a heavenly life that is unchanging and eternal. In heaven, our soul's only desire is to be closer to God, because love is the strongest force that unites. That is why, once you accept Jesus in your heart, you can begin to fulfill your mission on earth by serving Him, so that when you are in heaven you may be that much closer to Him. Death is the mid-point on a cyclical journey. Death is like the waking up point; while birth is when we go to sleep to dream this life we live.

> *Live so that thou mayest desire to live again—that is thy*
> *duty—for in any case thou wilt live again!"*
> *—Freidrich Nietzsche*

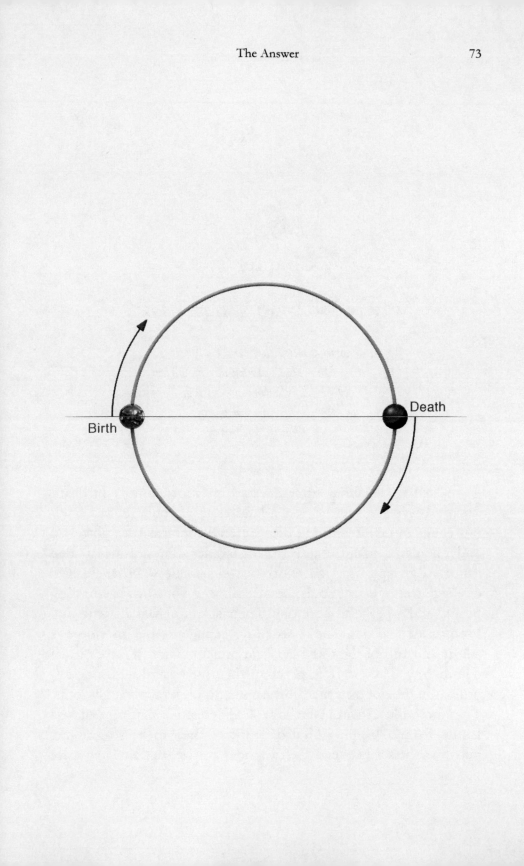

Chapter 7

Where Do I Go When I Die?

Our birth is but a sleep and a forgetting;
The Soul that rises with us, our life's Star,
Hath had elsewhere its setting.
And cometh from afar.
—William Wordsworth

When I was about fifteen, I had my most important death dream. I was a spectator over a landscape of souls. It was obvious to me in my dream that they were all souls, as they glistened and undulated in an ethereal transparency. They were divided into two groups, with an enormous chasm between them. On one side were perfect souls, beings shining with bright blinding beauty and a peaceful harmony. Their splendor was devastating, both inside and out. They needed no explanation. This side was sunny and full of light and laughter and I got the sense of great community. They were at peace in themselves and with one another. On the opposite side of the great divide were the ugly souls. They were like Edvard Munch's "The Scream" painting, but in a frothy, foamy, dripping kind of vomit. (Sorry to be so graphic, but the contrast between the two sides was extreme.) They were repulsive, worse that any Hollywood horror movie creature or nightmare fantasy. Their side of the chasm was overcast and cold, with a desolate, unforgiving landscape of jagged grey rock. They focused forlornly across the void at the beautiful souls. The only unifying factors in this group were a desperate longing and deep dissatisfaction with their own state of being. They were in love, because the kind of core beauty that existed across the void attracted them undeniably. But the separation between the two groups was insurmountable.

On the ugly side of the great valley stood an enormous revolving door and an endless line of ugly souls had formed, waiting to pass through it. As I watched, ugly souls passed into the revolving door and instantaneously re-emerged, most of them seemed slightly improved. Each time they went through, they came right back out a little more beautiful, a degree lighter, an iota more winsome. On occasion, a soul exited and was improved enough to be reclassified as (breathtakingly) beautiful, or perfect. It was immediately transported, its great weightlessness, joy and radiance lifting it high above the chasm, to fly across and join into parity with the other beautiful souls on the other side of the valley.

As I watched one flutter away from my side I noticed Jesus, transcendent, standing on the opposite rim of the canyon, with arms outstretched to welcome the new soul coming home to Him. He was smiling, glowing, overjoyed to greet the newly transfigured soul.

The beautiful souls are one with God, in Heaven.

We are the souls that need purification in order to join with God, on the other side of the great chasm. The revolving door is this world, and our souls enter repeatedly, as they wish, just for the opportunity to someday soar across to the other side.

For our light and momentary troubles are achieving for us
an eternal glory that far outweighs them all.
(2 Cor 4:17)

Woven as the fabric of this universe are the Laws of Balance, Polarity, Cause and Effect, Circulation and Resonance. The only thing outside of these laws is God Himself, who is also outside of time and matter. We are shackled by time, which distorts our perceptions because it prevents us from viewing the entire picture. Time is like a view-finder on a camera. There is so much that happens outside the frame. A pendulum that is swung out at 28 degrees may appear to be simply 28 degrees from center, but the real story lies in how fast and which way it is currently moving. If you only see late fall, bare trees and all their orange, yellow and brown leaves rotting on the ground, you might easily conclude that the end of the earth is near. To realize the balance of life we must explore the entire revolution of the earth, the whole year, and understand its cyclical nature.

I look upon death to be as necessary to the constitution as sleep.
We shall rise refreshed in the morning.
—Benjamin Franklin

Christ lived and died about 2000 years ago. We have recorded human history of less than 6000 years. Scientists have established that the earth is around four-and-a-half billion years old and the universe is about fourteen billion years old. Our imaginations cannot really grasp those figures because, generally, humans exist in 100-year intervals. To refer to prehistoric times we say "a long, long, long time ago." Our meager science cannot offer any explanation for before the big bang, because it was a singularity, the moment when time began. Scientists have postulated that the universe is expanding. The prediction is that at some point it will begin to slowly collapse back in on itself again. Basically they liken it to the universe breathing. We are living during an inhalation. The reality we are facing is so much greater than we can possibly grasp. With all the research and calculations we have, we still come up with a vast unknown and incomprehensible universe and creator. The best thing we can hope for is to accept that there is an immeasurable amount of information and knowledge that our meager human minds and strained imaginations will never be able to know. It is as if we are puppies at the foot of a desk on which sits a computer. A puppy can relate to a computer probably about as well as we can understand the true nature of this universe and our role in it. We must simplify the universe into something relevant and reasonable to us, but in doing so we are obliged to recognize that our complete comprehension of it is compromised.

> *As long as you are not aware of the continual law of Die and*
> *Be Again, you are merely a vague guest on a dark Earth.*
> *—Johann Wolfgang von Goethe*

As Goethe believed, death and life are like sleeping and being awake. Problems are not solved in sleep, so if you depart this earth leaving issues of the soul unresolved, you shall find the same challenges when you return to life. Inside that circuit, when we walk this planet, we have opportunity to grow and stretch, to make ourselves better and work on the fabric of our souls. Christ said that we would reap what we sow, and this world is ultimately fair and just. Even if we cannot see it in the viewfinder right now, we will harvest the fruits of our labors, of our actions, eventually. We choose to come into this world of our own free will, to do the hard work to improve our souls to be worthy of God.

Death is not a severance from your soul's obligations.

Death seems like the ultimate loss. If you are lucky enough to live a long life, then by the time death is knocking you have already lost youth and beauty; your children have moved away and your parents are gone. The moment you die, you transcend over to the other side and realize that everything you thought was lost is there in eternity: life, beauty, and loved ones. Of course, the material things are gone, but they have no worth in heaven. Loss of earthly things is no loss. The soul keeps its most valuable possessions through every transition, through karma and the power of love. What you go to your death with is what you will revisit in your next life, just like the world when you go to sleep is the same world when you wake up. Do not expect that your estranged father will embrace you when you wake up, or that your empty bank account will be replenished overnight. Karma applies the same way to our lives. Life has an incredible logic. The night does not separate you from your responsibilities from the day before.

> *God generates beings,*
> *and sends them back over and over again,*
> *till they return to Him.*
> *(Koran)*

Death is not the end; suicide is no answer. In German, the word for suicide, *selbstmord*, translates into "self-murder," which better describes the act than the more ambiguous English word. Murder is murder, after all, and all life is sacred. Even with faith in the other side, faith that heaven is like a Garden of Eden, we must also appreciate that to depart an unresolved life is simply to leave a mess for the next one.

When you factor in eternal karma, suicide is no escape.

We live in order to improve our souls, to become more perfect and loving. Taking your own life is robbing yourself of the great opportunity of this existence. Since living is so challenging, the choice to come alive could not possibly be one made on a whim. The rewards must equal the efforts. It must be absolutely incredible to propel us to take on the suffering and hardship that life encompasses. To freely squander the gift of life by self-murder, well, that is true tragedy. The suicide victim has punished himself in the gravest way, by burdening his soul with this crime, and removing himself further from the presence of his loving God. He has meaningfully turned away from God.

Jesus taught the law of divine justice:

> *"In anger his master turned him over to the jailers until he*
> *should pay back all he owed. This is how my heavenly Father*
> *will treat each of you unless*
> *you forgive your brother from your heart."*
> *(Matthew 18: 34-35)*

But Jesus didn't invent divine justice; it also appears in the Old Testament:

> *Life for life, eye for eye, tooth for tooth, hand for hand, foot*
> *for foot, burn for burn, wound for wound, bruise for bruise."*
> *(Exodus 21:24-25)*

The fact is, this law, this assumption, has existed throughout history. It can be equated with karma, and it implies, of course, reincarnation. Only reincarnation can explain the divine justice that we yearn for—the explanation that life is fair, people get their due and reap what they sow. It explains, though only to a certain degree, why some are born into favor and others, hardship.

The universal law of balance with its pendulums gives us the surety of karma, divine justice—the recognition that everything is cyclical. What, then, of the injustice we *perceive*? What of the evil man who lives a long and happy life, cheating others or worse? Where is the justice in that? Where is his karma?

Try, try, and try again.

The only way that any of our life on earth makes sense is to acknowledge that there is more than meets the eye, and that we return to this life repeatedly. Without the possibility of revisiting to finish what we started in this lifetime, the karma we each set into action, there is no possible balance, the Law of Cause and Effect would no longer apply, and life truly would not be fair. But we have already absolutely concluded that Cause and Effect, Balance and Justice prevail. And so we must be afforded ample opportunity to "get it right."

- **re·in·car·na·tion;** Pronunciation: \ˌrē-(ˌ)in-(ˌ)kär-ˈnā-shən\
- Function: *noun* ; Date: 1845
- From ecclesiastical Latin *incarnatus,* past participle of *incarnari* ('"be made flesh'"), from in- + caro ('"flesh'"), with re ("again")
  1 a : the action of reincarnating : the state of being reincarnated
  b : rebirth in new bodies or forms of life; *especially* : a rebirth of a soul in a new human body
  2 : a fresh embodiment[6]

Origen Adamantius (c.185–c.254) was, for many, the first theologian of the Christian Church. He is still today considered an early church father. He spent his entire life devoted to the study of and teaching from the Bible. Though his works no longer exist in their entirety (he was a prolific writer), what remains of *De Principiis,* perhaps his greatest theological work, indicates an understanding about the preexistence of souls and reincarnation, which was not an original concept for early Christianity.

WHAT HAPPENS TO OUR SOULS WHEN WE DIE?

When you return from a long trip away, and you get home and open the door, what happens? Your loved ones make a special effort to welcome you. Your father or mother or spouse rushes to the door to greet you. Your children run up and tackle your legs. The same thing is true when we pass from this world into the next. Loved ones who were no longer in life greeted Don Piper with tremendous song and joyousness, at what he described as marvelous entry gates (which he never entered.) In no case did he see, in death, anyone who was still alive. In many near-death reports, people have related similar experiences of seeing loved ones who had died before them. Homecomings are joyous events, to be celebrated with love and elation.

For in that sleep of death what dreams may come,
When we have shuffled off this mortal coil,
Must give us pause.
—William Shakespeare's Hamlet

Once we have seen God, we want to become God-like with all our might. That is the driving force behind every human being you see walking around on this earth. Our ignorance of our past lives does not erase them. There are documented studies of people suddenly recollecting things of which they had no previous awareness, speaking in languages they had never heard in their lifetime. How can that happen? Because whether you remember them or not, things that have impacted you soul continue to do so. They do not just haphazardly disappear. Your soul carries their imprints. Piano lessons are forgotten in detail, but the effects of the lessons stay with you to create the pianist that you become. It is the same in our lives. Rest assured that much of what comes to you in this life results directly from what you have done before, whether in this life or another one.

There is an unquestionably positive side to forgetting. Roger Federer, for instance, is certainly not traumatized by all the early mistakes that he made on the tennis court. Most likely, he remembers very few of them because they have become irrelevant to the master tennis player Federer has grown into today. Making those mistakes benefited him, cumulatively, such that he developed into an expert tennis player, so their individual memories no longer serve a purpose. In fact, it is good he has forgotten them, since recollection of all of them today would undoubtedly impair his game. The same thing holds true for us. With time on earth, we get better and better. We may still make mistakes, but because we are programmed to learn through our mistakes, face the resistance, and thus grow, any blunders become tools for self-improvement. Errors are necessary, and Federer could not have become Federer without making his mistakes on the tennis court when he set out to learn tennis. In fact, it is because of those missteps that he is who he is today, and it is because of the errors we make that we are given the chance to grow through times of adversity. Although we often have no choice in the problems that come our way, the option that will never be taken from us is how we react to our circumstances.

If we equate God with love, we must allow that love can penetrate the boundaries of time and matter.

Love transcends time, which means that loving relationships can endure beyond the earthly grave much like Jesus, once risen from the dead, returned to his disciples to reaffirm His connection with them.

Have you ever used the phrase "we just clicked?" Why would that happen, without some external/internal influence? It is the Holy Spirit that is orchestrating those moments. If someone you love dies and is reborn, you will not instantly recognize them, but you will perceive, intrinsically, the relationship that once was. You recognized each other, not physically, because you never met in this lifetime, but by love, and by the Law of Resonance.

A man and a woman meet and feel immediately at ease with each other, like they have known each other all their lives. They have each found their soul mate, because their spirits have recognized each other. The fit is good and true, and they marry. The man goes to work in the morning, leaving his wife for the entire day, but when he returns at night everything is as he left it, and the relationship continues. Perhaps there is an argument, but that does not affect the deep level of commitment in the pair, because love will not allow it.

Love is always selfless.

It is not a business deal whereby if you love well enough you get rewarded. That would be an intellectual decision. No—love is its own reward. That does not imply that it is smart or even fair. It is beyond those qualities.

Love is the immense power that unites.
Hatred is the great power that divides.

The opposite of love is the destructive force of hatred. Hatred is also a very powerful force and for that reason it is also timeless. Have you ever met someone you just did not like? There was no obvious reason behind it but there was an impasse, a block on your feelings of acceptance or friendship for this person. That, too, may be your soul speaking to you and referencing a past hurt. Perhaps you do not recognize them, but your spirit does, and your spirit rejects them. You may be conflicted, because you have no rational reason to despise them so powerfully. There is no history there that you remember but the memory has no relevance here. Your spirit understands the nature of your relationship with that person.

The physical law of conservation of mass-energy states simply that the total energy and mass in a closed system is constant. Nothing is created or destroyed, for instance, in a nuclear explosion. Mass is turned into energy. Consider that! Even in a nuclear explosion, we see destruction on a human level, but on a cosmic level, we are just transforming mass into energy, its equivalent. Conservation of mass-energy applies just as easily to our souls.

Going back to your personal memories, they have no real importance when compared to the energy between you and the other being. Like a printing press and its newspaper, once the paper is printed the press is expendable and, in fact, they break it down and reuse it to print tomorrow's paper. But the paper remains, to inform and guide, and shows the proof of the existence of the press that printed it. Well, if someone imprinted a bad deed on your soul, and if it was strong enough, the impression would last, even when you meet him or her in another lifetime. Just like when you love someone, if the hurt was performed yesterday or a thousand years ago, the energy behind the injury remains to inform you. Karma.

> *So we fix our eyes not on what is seen, but on what is unseen.*
> *For what is seen is temporary,*
> *but what is unseen is eternal.*
> *(2 Corinthians 4:18)*

We are conditioned to see with our eyes and touch with our hands in order to verify, but our perceptions are tragically limited by time, by our capacity to comprehend, and by our imaginations. It is useful to reflect back on the laws of the universe and examine how they set the stage for our understanding of karma. We are like children climbing an enormous ladder. Each rung is an obstacle, selected by cause and effect. It is possible to get stuck on one rung for a while, but eventually we will reach the top of the ladder.

Once we are born, the only thing that is certain is that we will die. The most obvious assumption, based on all the examples of circuitry that we have in this universe, is that when we die, we are assured that we will be reborn. One side cannot exist without the other.

Which came first, the chicken or the egg?

The chicken implies the egg, and the egg presages the chicken. The only one who is outside of this cycle, outside of time, outside the laws of the universe, is God. So He is the only exclusion to these laws.

Developing conscience is a final step in our evolution, and it seems also to reflect a distancing from the physical body. For instance, many animals winter outdoors because they have fur that protects them. Any human who would try to winter in freezing temperatures would have a quick trip to the morgue. Humans used to be cave-people, hardy and tough, but not anymore. As we become more intellectual, more aware, we become less physical and weaker in our bodies. The higher evolved we are, the more spiritual we become. It is an awakening from the animal world, into the human world, and finally over to the spiritual world. Once you recognize death for what it is, there is nothing to fear. Death is the easiest thing you will ever do.

> *When we are born, we cry and everyone else laughs.*
> *When we die we laugh while everyone else cries.*
> *—Old Greek saying*

THE PROMISE AND THE RECKONING

Jesus promised that you shall reap what you sow: karma. He also assured us of the Day of Judgment, when all souls will stand before God and their accounts will be reconciled. The Judgment Day is distinct from your death day, because you are not afforded two trials. There are not two individual verdicts. The Final Reckoning takes place when Jesus returns, and then your soul, after many lifetimes and many trials, will stand before God and know its fate.

As we live through thousands of dreams in our present life,
so is our present life only one of many thousands of such lives,
which we enter from the other more real life and then return
after death. Our life is but one of the dreams of
that more real life, and so it is endlessly,
until the very last one, the very real life of God.
—Count Leo Tolstoy

Life has much more meaning, once you realize that *life* encompasses the entire life-and-death cycle. There is Heaven and there is Hell and there is also Purgatory. Purgatory is the life-death cycle. There is not a Purgatory that is separate from life-on-Earth. Earthly life is part of the Purgatory referred to in the Bible. Why would there be a fourth sphere? Is the unabashed defrauder relaxing in Purgatory waiting for Judgment Day? Is the shameless killer biding his time in Purgatory, thinking up excuses? No. They are fulfilling their respective karmas here in this world, atoning for past mistakes and benefitting from the opportunity to change their ways, afforded them by an all-loving, all-forgiving Almighty.

Reincarnation is the only way to logically explain the three spheres of existence referred to in the Bible and the (otherwise) "senselessness" of life.

The more spiritually aware you become, the less you fear death.

Chapter 8

Is There Heaven and Is There Hell?

My life closed twice before its close;
It yet remains to see
If Immortality unveil
A third event to me,
So huge, so hopeless to conceive,
As these that twice befell.
Parting is all we know of heaven,
And all we need of hell.
—Emily Dickenson

This life is a purification process our souls choose, in order to better experience God. God will guide us, but the work at hand is ours alone.

The other side of the cycle: heaven and hell.

Through studying the signature of God (nature), we have an inkling of what happens after this life: it is the night to our day. Purgatory is the life-death cycle. Once God passes His final judgment, our souls will be shown into either heaven or hell, and the work that we've done incarnate will be rewarded.

HEAVEN

In heaven, everything is constant, and neither time nor matter exists. Heaven is entirely spiritual. You cannot lose your life. You cannot lose your health, or your love. You cannot lose anything. There is no beginning or end in heaven, because there is no time. In heaven there is the principle of unity, whereas here on earth we have the law of polarity. In heaven all is one and one is all. Like a violinist who has no solo, your soul will play in the body of the orchestra, where all the musicians perform as a single unit. The orchestra is heaven. In order to enter the heavenly symphony, you must pass a rigorous screening process known as life on earth, because in heaven there are no mistakes. Heaven is God's realm, so there is no deceit, no lies, no evil. There is only absolute purity and complete perfection. Otherwise, it would not be heaven. The place we call heaven is the exact antidote to the earthly pain that we have experienced in this world. All the pain that we freely took upon ourselves here on earth in order to achieve heaven is relieved and replaced by blessed love and peace.

Heaven is the place that God inhabits together with all the souls that have become God-like. It is not a better world. It is not a world we can even begin to imagine. It is entirely unearthly. Heaven actually happens in an entirely different (and humanly incomprehensible) dimension. It has a different purity, where not even the slightest bad or negative thought could ever exist.

Heaven means to be one with God.
—Confucius

But because we are human and inquisitive, here is the best analogy I have for the structure of heaven: There is a hierarchy of purity, like a pyramidal staircase. Our souls sit on stairs of varying degrees of righteousness. The more pure you become, the closer to the top, the nearer to God you can sit. It is an eternal ecstasy of love.

Imagine all the pain of this life, and all lives before, and all universes and put them on one side of a scale. What we experience in heaven is the great equalizer to all this suffering in one eternal moment.

God is the singularity, or summit, with all our souls settling around him on the vast, staircase, wanting to be near to Him but not being pure enough to reach the summit. Like magnets that are drawn toward the North Pole, our souls wait, fixed in their various levels of purity. When a soul is truly pure, it is absorbed into God the Singularity, in unity and love. In this analogy, God, at the top of the stairs, is heaven.

Compare a black-and-white still photo with a high definition video. We live in a world of stagnant black and white. We are tied to a human level, the human experience, which is drastically limited by our human perceptions. Try describing a high-definition 3-D color video with audio to a deaf and blind person. We on earth are deaf and blind to the magnificence of heaven, so our best approximation must be "beyond description."

Heaven-born, the soul a heavenward course must hold;
beyond the world she soars; the wise man, I affirm,
can find no rest in that which perishes,
nor will he lend his heart to ought that doth time depend.
—Michelangelo

Being the opposite of heaven, on Earth everything changes all the time, and therefore there is opportunity for our souls to become more pure and closer to God. Through life on earth and our own free will, God supplies us with unlimited chances to improve our own state in His eyes. The sad thing is that a few of us will inevitably reject God repeatedly and determinedly, and God will eventually accept that decision in eternity.

ETERNITY

Eternity is not a long time, or even a very long time. Eternity is the absence of time. Eternal damnation means separation forever from God. It is not a punishment. It is a simple screening process to keep impurity out of heaven. Heaven is not a better place than earth; it is only a different dimension of purity, which we are barred from entering until we are prepared in our souls.

Knowing the Kingdom of Heaven and knowing God, and then being eternally separated from Him; that is Hell.

HELL

Classical painters depict hell as devils and fire, teeth gnashing and souls crying out for mercy and relief from great physical pain. It was the best they could do, because, like heaven, hell is also another dimension that defies human-based description. But if you have ever been in love and been rebuffed, you know that the pain of unrequited love can seem worse than physical pain. There is no aspirin for it. Escape from consciousness is the only reprieve. The throbbing of heartache is unrelenting. Its hopelessness is devastating. Multiply that by infinity, (the measure of God's love) and what do you have? Absolute misery. What is a better representation for the unimaginable pain of knowing you have forsaken a God who loves you infinitely, and will be in all eternity alone and without Him, your one true love? Upon reflection, even the most horrific scenes of human suffering are not enough to convey the wretched despair that eternal damnation would be. Torture, fire and suffering are the best interpretations of the agony of an unreciprocated love of God, combined with self-condemnation. It is the end of the end. It is final nothingness, but not the atheistic version. There is an exacting consciousness of absolute loss with no hope for reprieve: spiritual fatality.

Iron Mike Tyson served three years in prison. After his recent release, he described his experience as "hellish." Everyone hated. Loathing reverberated off the walls. There was no escape. Hatred and desperation were the essence of this jail and he thought only of returning to society. In an interview, he recounted how unnerved and intimidated he was by the patent evil of that dark place. This was a boxer who bit off someone's ear in the ring; this was "Iron Mike" talking.

Believe it or not, Tyson's prison is the kids' version of Hell. In Hell, you are given an endless sentence, with no hope for parole, not even through death. You are surrounded by other souls that are beyond redemption as their crimes were horrendous and they never sought forgiveness. Hell is a jail term of eternity, devoid of hope and love but seething with contempt and despair. Welcome to eternal damnation.

God warns us over and over again not to take the wrong path, a path from which there is no return. How unbearably painful it must be for Him to watch His child suffering in that way. How dreadful to be that wayward soul in eternal separation from God, facing the putrid loathing and accumulated evils of this world in eternity. Truly this understanding alone should make any thinking person shudder and redouble their own efforts to search for the truth, the good, and the light.

> *The hottest places in Hell are reserved for those who in*
> *time of great moral crises maintain their neutrality.*
> *—Dante Alighieri*

Love is like water. You can have an ocean of water or only a glass or only a drop, but the substance of it is still wet. It permeates and soaks you. Have a gulp, and you will want more. Without it, you will wither. Where human love is like a bottle-full or a shower, God's love is all the oceans combined. It is unending, unfathomable. Standing on the shore and looking out into the ocean, you can hardly comprehend its expansiveness, or its fathomless depths. It is unreserved and unconditional. The ocean of God's love looks back at you with no preset expectations or reprobation. It is the ocean. You are a small thing in comparison. It sees you entirely for who you are, and it waits patiently for you to come in.

In this life, we struggle to achieve the things we want. We attend university to get a good job to make money to buy things. Nobody wants to work hard to earn money in order to give it all away. No one goes to medical school for years on end without the intent of practicing medicine. We labor through hardship in order to obtain something in return. This is the work/reward principle. Our efforts in this life, on behalf of our souls, are rewarded in heaven by the same principle. Think of all the pains in this world, not only this lifetime, but from all lifetimes. This amount is more than any of us could ever imagine, greater than all the grains of sand on all the beaches of the world. Take all the pain that all creatures ever went through and put it on one side of a scale. On the other tray, place all the joy, so much happiness and rejoicing as to equal all that pain and hardship. That is the bliss that awaits you on the other side, and your soul took on this world freely because it knows what is waiting for you when you return. The joys of heaven must truly be heavenly, and impossible for us to imagine, because they must balance the pain of this world that we freely take upon ourselves. Like a lover understanding he must complete certain tasks before his beloved will be with him fully, your soul is in love with God, willing to tackle any problem to prove your love, to be worthy of love. It is for that ultimate reward that any of us enter life: for being united with God in the unity of all, in heaven.

Perhaps they are not stars, but rather openings in heaven
where the love of our lost ones pours through and
shines down upon us to let us know they are happy.
—Eskimo Proverb

Heaven is the place where God resides. Each soul's goal is to get closer to God, because of the love He has placed within each of His creations. The more work we do to perfect our souls on this earthly plane, the closer we will be with God in heaven. It is a cycle, and it ends when, through grace, we are allowed to be with Him, in Heaven, or when He determines that we are beyond saving, and that is truly Hell.

The love of heaven makes one heavenly.
—William Shakespeare

Chapter 9

Is This World Just?

If God is Good,
He must be True.
If God is True,
He must be Just.

There cannot be goodness without justice and there is no justice without truth.

"Do we live in a just world?" is certainly one of the fundamental questions we face. The quick and dirty answer for this question is that obviously the world is not just, implying that God either does not exist at all, or if He does exist, perhaps He is like an absentee landlord. He lets His tenants work out their differences amongst themselves, ambivalent to any outcome. But that is all part of the fast answer, and if we give this question of justice a little more thought, we can find a more satisfactory and more correct response.

Justice is cause and effect.

We have already seen that God does indeed exist, and that He is the very essence of goodness. So, how do we reconcile fairness in this seemingly unjust world? There cannot be justice without truth, and there cannot be goodness without justice. Goodness, Truth and Justice are interconnected, and interdependent.

If God is good, then why is there evil at all?

Justice is a principle of this world. It is the cousin of balance and polarity. Our human shortcoming (one of them, anyway) is that we see this world through the prism of time, and we can only see one life at a time. An enormous pendulum swings both ways, but with our human myopia we can only see one side of it. We might have to wait a while before seeing it complete its cycle. Justice, like God, exists outside of time. Endeavoring to attach your concept of timing to it is like trying to tie a tail on a kite that is already aloft. For humans, 60 years is a long time (although if you ask many octogenarians, they will assure you it was only yesterday they graduated high school). For a butterfly that lives for a single week, 60 years is too much time to fathom. Justice is eternal.

What is 60 years, or a lifetime, to eternity?

Whatever you put out into this world has an effect back on you. Nothing is lost. You cannot think one bad thought without its associated consequences to yourself. You certainly cannot do anything, good or bad, without affecting your surroundings, which then have some effect on your soul. In the end, you are always looking into a mirror.

The universe is completely balanced.

It is not only partly balanced. That would be like being a little pregnant: impossible! Our world is 100 percent balanced. We are challenged to perceive justice because it is distorted by time. Like a light that, when shone through a prism, becomes the entire rainbow, time also warps our vision and makes things appear out of equilibrium. If I show you the refracted light on the wall, but I only show you the red portion, you will think I only have a red light. Go back to the source, and see that the light is bright white, but it is separated into its compositional colors by the prism. All the colors are there, in balance; and in life, all the stories are there with the soul, but the prism of time lets us see only the story of this lifetime, or this particular situation.

There are two sides to every story.

Picture a prison and two of its prisoners. One is due for release in a year, while another is incarcerated for life. How unfair it is for one man to be imprisoned so much longer than the other one! And what of the judge? It is easy to fault the judge for sentencing the two men so disproportionately. One side of the story always seems unjust. Two sides reveal the balance. The prisoners' full stories illustrate the judge's impartiality in sentencing. The first prisoner got caught holding up a gas station, and the second one killed another man in cold blood. Suddenly, life seems fair again.

Life is fair. Justice rules.

Trust in the Laws of Cycles, Cause and Effect and Balance. I do not have to know both sides to understand the cycle ensures they are both present.

JUSTICE

Of course, human judges are not infallible; quite the contrary, unfortunately. But the analogy is sound. You cannot necessarily see outside of life's prison to what actions preceded your punishments, but the infallible judge of justice rules with impartiality, ultimate clarity and perfect reason, and individual consequences derive from causative behavior. Let me be clear that I am not referring to God as the judge here. He does not punish. The Law of Cause and Effect does that autonomously. God only set the ground rules with His morality and His goodness. Then He gave us free will, such that a moral and good justice may be served impartially upon us for our choices.

Justice, as it is served in its own time, is a reflection of free will.

Everything has an origin. The origins are all within us, within our thoughts, our souls, and our decisions. We bring our decisions out into the world. They interact or find conflict out there, and eventually they come back to us.

Justice is truth in action.
—Benjamin Disraeli

Imagine: There is a nice guy who lived next door to you for the last year. He generously helped with your lawnmower and collected your mail while you were visiting your sick mother. Is it fair that the police came to arrest him? He seemed so very sweet, right? Yes, he was very kind to you, but his late wife, whom he killed, may beg to differ. My point here is that you simply cannot know the whole story. When bad things happen to good people there is a reason; and often it remains obscured.

EVIL

Negative experiences, like a car accident, illness, financial loss or other problems, are opportunities for our souls to mature. They may not seem fair at the time, but only because we cannot see the bigger picture. For eons, people have naïvely argued that God cannot be good and just, using as proof the evils we witness each day. What this reasoning fails to recognize is twofold. First, evil is just goodness in relief. Polarity. In other words, without evil there could be no good; there would be nothing.

The absence of evil is not goodness.

Second, simply because you do not know a strategy does not imply that it is lacking. It only means you are not capable enough to appreciate it.

It is easier to say that the existence of evil precludes the existence of God, than it is to say that all the goodness in the world is undeniable proof of God.

The argument that an apparent lack of justice would disprove God is specious and juvenile. It is akin to a child who does not like the punishment for his misbehaving, saying, "You're not my father." The punishment, or correction, serves to guide the child toward more proper or safer behavior. Disciplining is a necessary part of raising children. Because our Father is present and He is good, we obviously must be misunderstanding the nature of evil and of justice to make many of the arguments there.

There are two types of evil: moral evil, where man commits evil acts upon other men, and amoral evil such as tornadoes and hurricanes. The guilt of any moral evil is born entirely by man. Man, with free will, acts according to his own choices, and therefore we can hardly blame God for injuries brought on us by each other. We must all suffer the consequences of our choices, be they for the good or for bad.

Amoral evils, on the other hand, are things like accidents or extreme weather. They are neutral, with no rationale behind them, save the hidden agenda of nature or justice. This agenda is born of cause and effect, although we may call them "acts of God." They are simply the consequential fulfillment of nature's inescapable laws.

FREE WILL

When justice is meted out immediately, free will is eclipsed. No rational person would try to embezzle from their boss if there was certainty that the police would handcuff him as he exited the building. That is why surveillance video cameras can be so effective. The would-be shoplifter looks up to see a camera and, fearing immediate repercussions, she leaves the store wearing only what she came in with. Her free choice was substantially limited by the threat of instant and direct consequences. In the larger picture, there are many ways to cheat in this life, many moral challenges to face. Your decisions precisely affect your soul, which is what you are here to perfect. If justice is always immediate, where is the moral dilemma? It disappears into the rationale for self-preservation. It is the prospect of getting away with doing the bad thing that makes it possible for us to choose between right and what we know is wrong.

Remove the proximity of the adjudicator to better challenge the soul to stay pure.

Free choice has everything to do with feeling undetected. Most of us feel invisible to an ultimate judging mechanism. Out of sight, out of mind. Even though many of us believe in God, we often do things that are not moral or that conflict with our own conscience because we are seduced by the possibilities. We can easily suspend our fear of consequences because we believe there is no concrete proof of justice in our world. Not only that, it often appears that bad people are rewarded handsomely. Thus we may rationalize, we may make up excuses, but ultimately we know there is no excuse for bad behavior.

If we always felt like actors on stage, and our every move was witnessed by an audience, none of us would do harm to anyone else. It is only because we think our actions have no consequences that we try to get away with doing what we know is wrong. We are free to do good or evil, but don't mistake freedom with unaccountability. We are always accountable, even without a witness.

But deliver us from evil
–The Lord's Prayer

In Mark Twain's story, "The Man Who Corrupted Hadleyburg," a stranger comes to a small town that is known as the "most honest and upright town in all the region around about." The motto of this little town is "Lead Us Not Into Temptation," a well-known phrase from the Lord's Prayer. Throughout the story, the stranger discovers in the town's inhabitants each of their weakest traits, and he sets about to reveal their hypocrisy as he ensnares them. This is easily done because they openly boast about their virtues. Eventually, he lays ruin to the reputations of the townspeople, by systematically luring them out of their self-righteousness into sin, be it greed or simple dishonesty. In the end, the town changes its motto to "Lead Us Into Temptation," because the townspeople realize that without any temptations to resist, they were never tested, and therefore any claims they made of honesty and integrity were only empty promises.

The more difficult the triumph, the more valuable the return.

Doing the right thing is a challenge, remaining righteous in the face of temptation, but nothing worth having is ever gotten easily. Removing justice to be served in its own time and place, allows for Free Will.

Mark had an older brother, Ben. The boys' mother designated Ben as trustee of her estate, whereby upon her death, her entire estate went to Ben to manage on behalf of both of the sons. There was never any doubt by anyone intimately connected with the family that the estate would be amicably and equally divided after Mark came of age to inherit his share. But when the time came for Mark to receive his portion, Ben denied the existence of the trustee agreement. He declared that he was perplexed by his mother's actions in leaving everything to him, but that Mark was obviously not to be trusted, and therefore deserved nothing. He came up with many excuses for not fulfilling his obligations but, simply put, he just wanted the money.

What is hateful to you, do not to your fellow;
that is the whole Law;
all the rest is interpretation.
–Talmud

Mark was understandably furious and devastated when he learned of the inconceivable betrayal. Of course, he held his brother accountable. He sued and pursued justice in the eyes of the law. Then he let go of the anger, and gave it up to cosmic Justice and God, because he understood there exists a bigger picture than the one revealed in this world. What Ben did will equally come back to him, like a pendulum. This is unavoidable. Mark and Ben are both poor souls, each on their own path to God, and they are both prone to mistakes. But with his duplicity, whether he understands this principle or not, Ben has certainly made the way more difficult for himself. Ben will not escape the justice he has demanded with his purposefully wicked choices. The funny thing is, if something bad happens to him, Ben will likely say, "How can God permit this?" He invited it, from the inescapable Law of Cause and Effect and from Justice herself.

> *The foundation of justice is good faith.*
> *—Marcus Tullius Cicero*

As for Mark, he must assume that his experience of this betrayal traces from somewhere within himself, in his soul's history, and that is how he finds the patience to forgive his brother. He does not hold himself to blame, per se, but he holds himself accountable on the spiritual plane. For this reason, he calms and shies from blaming God or even his brother. Ben's treachery only reached Mark because Mark was open to it.

Desire trumps reason.

You accidentally receive an extra five dollars in change at the grocery store. You know it is not yours but cannot resist the temptation to keep it because you won't get caught. The cashier does not know, and will not discover the mistake until it is too late to attach it to you. You rationalize that the grocery store is such a big business; nobody will miss a measly five bucks. The practical consequence, however, is that you must deal with your conscience telling you that you did a bad thing in keeping the excess change. That internal argument, self-condemnation/rationalization plays endlessly, at least until a bigger distraction comes along. God is found inside that moral dilemma, in the principles that discern right from wrong. God's voice declares the bad thing and urges you to give the money back, to "come clean." Why do we use the phrase "come clean?" Because the truth purifies by lifting the weight of the guilt from your shoulders. A small voice of justice launches in the oppression of the squabble inside your head over right and wrong. That 'free' five dollars never comes for free.

Truth cleanses the soul.

REACTIVE LIVING

Most of us live a life of reactions. If we get hungry, we eat. When we are tired, we sleep. For distraction, we go to a bar … Very few people live a conscious life (creative living) meaning that they are consciously trying to improve upon themselves and positively 'create' their souls. That is a true struggle, and who wants to struggle—life is hard enough, right? It seems easier to live reactively, because there is no initial expenditure. But that lifestyle removes us from the spiritual process we are here to experience. Life is emptier, inevitably, because reactive living has no purpose. Living reactively, you would more readily keep the five dollars. It is easier to justify taking that money when your agenda lacks morals or a search for God. You can defend keeping the money because you need it, you want it, or any other lame excuse.

I'll think about that tomorrow.
—Scarlett O'Hara in "Gone With the Wind"

Suspension of thought: ignoring the negative consequences of a behavior that offers immediate gratification, purposely not considering the consequences of an action.

We often persist in a behavior despite our knowing better, by merely refusing to contemplate it. For instance, I know I should not eat the entire ice cream sundae, although I am enjoying it. So, I purposely avoid thinking about the unpleasant part (why I should *not* finish the sundae) until I have polished it off. Then, it is too late to change the outcome. Afterward, I sit there, full, feeling not too great because I ate too much and also because I know in my heart I did not need to eat the whole thing. I am thinking, "Why did I do that?" But I know why—because I *wanted* it. It was not specifically amoral to eat myself silly (although gluttony is a sin, and for good reason!), but it was harmful to my body. Succumbing to rationalization or suspension of thought, immediate gratification will often win over logic.

CREATIVE LIVING

Political correctness has blurred the line between reactive living and creative living. It has been nurtured by our current "anything goes" mentality and the overall lack of integrity in society in general. *Suspension of thought* serves also to camouflage or distract from moral certitudes. If we were to earnestly contemplate our actions and thoughts on an ethical level and a spiritual plane, we would understand the implications of the evil we allow in our everyday lives. We are too often caught up in the rush to self-indulgence because of the spirit of these times, with the general public in a free-for-all of "what's in it for me?" It is, unfortunately, a downward, self-propelled spiral. By torpidly satisfying our desires regardless of eternal consequences, we believe we can find happiness, but our blind search for more is never completed because the state of more is unattainable. It is the selfish existence that prevents true happiness.

We ought always to deal justly, not only with those
who are just to us, but likewise to those who
endeavor to injure us; and this, for fear lest by rendering
them evil for evil, we should fall into the same vice.
—Hierocles

If the United States' founding fathers were alive today, they would be appalled by the banning of prayer in public schools as a consequence of "separation of church and state." They were all significantly religious men, as witnessed in the tremendous number of references to "God the Creator" in so many of their documents. "We hold these truths to be self-evident, that all men ... are endowed by their Creator with certain unalienable Rights ..." Of course, they would be astonished by the increasing lack of morals in society in general. Too, a society that has fallen away from God bristles at any reminder of how far they have fallen. Like a hopelessly overweight man throwing his scale out the window, certain factions of society are fighting endlessly for the removal of godly symbols that remind them of their eternal accountability.

The obese man will eventually reconcile his accounts by suffering from diabetes or heart failure. Justice will be served. Society will also pay in kind for its transgressions, but on a more esoteric scale. For every action there is a reaction. There are consequences to society's departure from God even as our increasing hedonism enlarges that distance. If we were truly on a path searching for God, we would not dream of keeping the five dollars of mistaken change at the store. Today, this simple choice appears to us as a reasonable moral dilemma. Would you drive at 90 MPH on a highway if you knew a cop was sitting behind the next bridge waiting with his radar gun? Of course not. But, if you were certain there were no cops? We would not dream of doing half the evil deeds we actually commit, let alone contemplate every day, if we were as certain of God and His laws as we ought to be. I hope with this book to change some of those circumstances.

This world is absolutely just. Justice is meted out under an eternal clock. Therefore, it is quite often invisible to the human eye, which is delimited by the human life span. But cause and effect is a law of the universe. Consequently, justice always applies.

With justice suspended outside of time, we are left with our free will and the ability to be tested as humans, in order to become stronger and develop more beautiful souls. Justice is applied and at force today, even if we cannot see it, much like gravity works invisibly. Gravity is immediate, and the consequences of defying the law of gravity can be, well, grave, indeed. But attempting to defy justice can result in equally dire results; nay, worse, I should say. Gravity is of this world and only physical, but Justice is timeless and eternal. We can fly, in spite of gravity, but we can do nothing outside the reach of Justice.

Do not believe that possibly you can
escape the reward of your action.
—Ralph Waldo Emerson

A good judge must be true, a true judge must be just

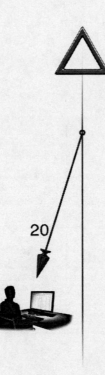

The Law of Cause and Effect: as authored by Christ in
the Sermon on the Mount
"Whatever you sow, so shall you reap."

A good judge must be true, a true judge must be just

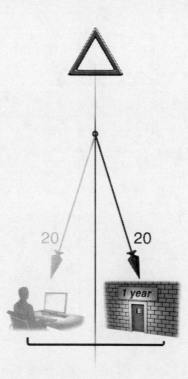

The Law of Cause and Effect: as authored by Christ in
the Sermon on the Mount
"Whatever you sow, so shall you reap."

A good judge must be true, a true judge must be just

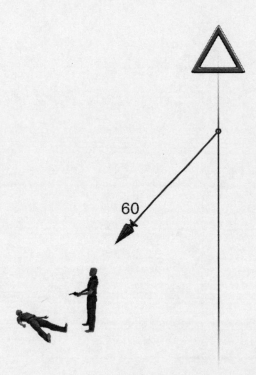

The Law of Cause and Effect: as authored by Christ in
the Sermon on the Mount
"Whatever you sow, so shall you reap."

A good judge must be true, a true judge must be just

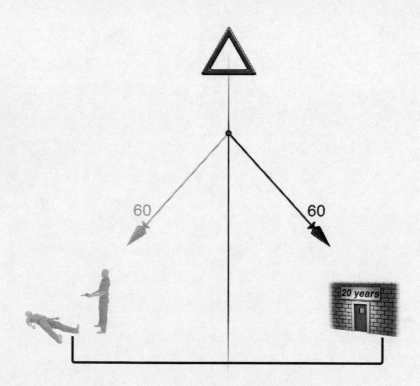

The Law of Cause and Effect: as authored by Christ in
the Sermon on the Mount
"Whatever you sow, so shall you reap."

Chapter 10

Why is There Suffering?

You desire to know the art of living, my friend?
It is contained in one phrase: make use of suffering.
—Henri-Frédéric Amiel

There are three categories of suffering.

- Karma
- The Test
- Carrying the Weight of Others

I heard a pastor recently who preached on the teachings of Jesus in the book of Luke. In the book, the crowd gathered wondered about people who experienced tragedy, like the Galileans who were murdered by Pilate or the tower of Siloam that fell and killed eighteen people. Were they being punished for their sins? In the text Jesus answers no, but then admonishes the crowd to repent of their own sins. The pastor summarized Jesus' message as recommending a "worry about yourself" attitude. This is admittedly troublesome for many. Basically, the "it's none of your business" approach falls a little short when all you can think is "WHY?" It seems a little hollow, although it isn't entirely wrong.

If God is good, why does he permit pain and suffering?

Whatever you send out into the world will come back to you. Yin and yang.

God gave you the gift of free choice, but because of the laws of the universe, your actions and your choices all have consequences: Polarity and Balance, Cause and Effect.

If you swing a pendulum out 30 degrees, it will swing back those 30 *and then 30 more*, an exact mirror image of the first thirty. It will not swing out 30, and then swing back down to rest, as if nothing had transpired. Instead, the result of the initial displacement will be an exact reflection of it. You cannot go through this world without leaving an imprint, which reflects back upon you. That is the basic Law of Cause and Effect, and it is always on, like gravity. Gravity does not take every other Friday off. It is at work every day and every minute of every day, even on your birthday. It is specific and constant. In fact, there is a numerical figure for gravity, which is the acceleration of 32 feet/second/second. This is known as the gravitational *constant* (meaning it does not change).

The Universal Laws by themselves are neither good nor bad; they are disinterested facts.

If you jump off the 23rd story of a building, gravity will arrange the terrible consequences. Equivalently, gravity is the wonderful magic that keeps you from quietly drifting off into space.

"A" is for apple …

I show you the letter "a" and I tell you it is part of the third page in chapter ten of a 600-page book. Better yet, I will give you the whole word: "about." Even if you know the plot line of the book, knowing one word helps nothing in comprehending the chapter or the story. You need most, if not all, of the words. There used to be a game show, "Name that Tune." The idea was to see if the contestant could guess the name of a song from just a few notes, or bars. Mind you, only songs that the contestant would reasonably have heard before were used. If I play you a note or a bar of a song you don't know, how can you possibly divine the song? You cannot. To think you can is presumptuous. To guess is presumptuous.

Judging a book by its cover.

You must take a step back (or several) and view the whole. To look at one frame of a movie, or even an entire scene, is not enough to judge the movie or whether the scene is true to the movie.

Apply this idea to your own life. When something bad happens to you or someone you love, it is very difficult to step back and see the whole picture, but without doing that, you are looking at a single word in a great book. You cannot view the entire picture or read the whole book. You have no distanced perspective of the event. This does not mean the thing that happened is not bad, but your judgment about its relevance or fairness is uninformed.

KARMIC SUFFERING

I met a young man once, Troy, who had suffered tremendously from a well-known disease that had gone undiagnosed a long time. Lyme disease masquerades with many confusing symptoms and is quite easily overlooked in a young teen. Troy had been exhibiting symptoms tracing back to when he was only 12, but they were thought to be normal "growing pains" and the like. He was a promising student at Cornell University when he began to feel very sickly, like he was losing his mind. The disease tricked him into believing he was going senile and dying. His recovery, severely compromised by the length he had harbored the disease prior to diagnosis, still remained uncertain three years later. He had endured intravenous antibiotics twice daily for months, was still on medication, and did not yet know if he would ever be able to finish college. Troy, then 21, told me that he had learned so much from the experience he would not trade it for anything. With hindsight, however, he saw the intrinsic value in the horrible thing that happened to him, and he chose the path of acceptance and gratitude, instead of anger and hurt.

Hindsight is just another word for perspective, which is what we mostly lack.

The universe has its own timeline, and once we are given the opportunity to see things from a distance, we come to understand the better nature of our challenges: how they made us stronger or wiser. The other option is to live in frustration, focusing on how things do not go "our way" and what is wrong in our world. This, of course, is the path toward misery.

> *... although the world is full of suffering,*
> *it is full also of the overcoming of it.*
> —*Helen Keller*[7]

For good or bad, we sentence ourselves the moment we do something, because like gravity, an effect exists for every cause. But because the passage of time often obscures the causal relationship of our circumstances, the manifestation of Cause and Effect on our actions goes undetected.

Time may well pass before a reaction to an action may be detected; a minute, a year, or many lifetimes, but nothing is lost in our universe. The universe does not forget. The question of the existence of God or any supreme judgmental being leaves open the possibilities for us to do as we please. We may betray our spouses, steal, lie or other things, and the possibility of no retribution makes us really choose between these evil deeds and taking the straight and narrow path. Children misbehave when the teacher leaves the room. With the teacher present, and seen, the naughtiness stops. God gave us free choice. He knows and sees, but he does not do so obviously, and therefore non-believers (and even weak believers) feel a freedom like children in a teacher-free classroom. There may be punishment later, but it is not an immediate threat, and it also is an unknown—might be bad, maybe not so bad—but the pull of the fun of mischief overcomes those pesky pangs of morality. With no discernible or imminent reprisals, we are left with only our own conscience to decide right from wrong, and God only gives us the compass.

People used to believe the earth was flat.

They fought for that belief, and condemned those who audaciously proposed our planet might be spherical. Just because it looked flat did not make that true, and just because your actions appear to have no adverse consequences does not make that the case.

Appearance is not reality.

The good and bad things you do today will swing back at you to the same degree as you perform or imagine them. This is the Law of Cause and Effect: the results of Free Will.

You stand before two pendulums. One represents evil, one represents good. Either pendulum will come back to you in equivalence. Push the good one, and goodness will swing back your way. Push the other, and you are asking for the same. When will the pendulums return? How long until they make the swing back of equal magnitude as the initial push, or action? The pendulum cares nothing for time or how it is measured. It swings on its own rhythm. Although it may seem like you pushed on something that moved away from you, not in an arch but just laterally, understand the pendulum is large enough that you cannot perceive that it is a swinging pendant. And the earth is not flat, but spherical.

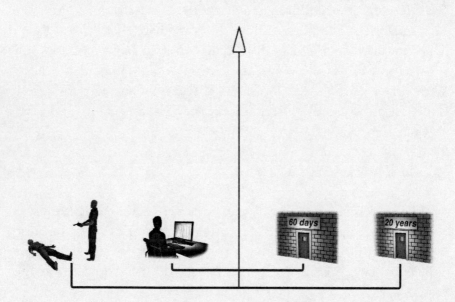

God is there, seeing all, and yet we are free to choose as we may, act of our own volition. It follows, then, that we are ultimately responsible for everything that happens in our lives. He is not going to be stepping in to muck things up now. Things that seem to make no sense, have no obvious precedence or reason, can most often be attributed to long lost actions from other times, or even other lives.

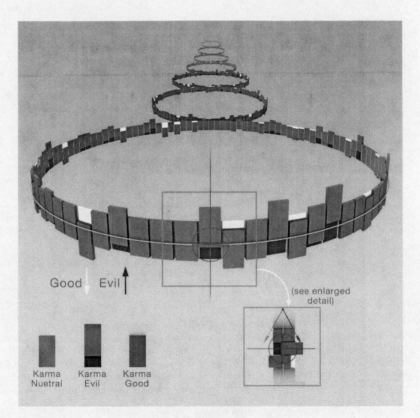

Good   Evil

(see enlarged detail)

Karma Nuetral   Karma Evil   Karma Good

THE KEY OF KARMA

The Key of Karma shows a circular band, with the present moment enlarged for clarity. Two forces, marked by the arrows "good" and "evil," push upon the malleable band, which represents our actions. Good presses down, while evil pushes up. These two forces are like gravity, constantly exerting pressure on us. Each moment of our lives gives us an opportunity to do either good or evil, and our responses produce impressions in the band, like the teeth seen in the diagram. The circularity of the band represents the fact that our 'response impression' will eventually come back around to us, whether it is in a moment or a day or a thousand years.

The impressions we leave in our karmic band—for good or for evil—will return to us in "Karmic Time."

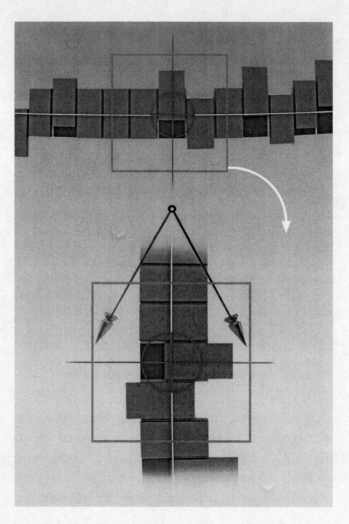

A child is given the problem "two plus two." He eventually discovers the answer is four. Perhaps he must try several times, perhaps he will not remember when he is asked again, or he repeats some mistakes when trying to solve it again. Eventually, he learns that two plus two is four each and every time. Once he uncovers and knows the answer, it releases the problem, and that equation is no longer a test for him. We all must face challenges, and we all learn from them before we can move on. While the child gets the answer wrong, for him this is a true dilemma, because he wants to be right. As we mature, the trials grow more complex, and so do the results from getting them wrong. God can forgive us, but the consequences of our mistakes are still there and must be faced, because of the Law of Cause and Effect. He can lighten the burden of them; make them easier to bear through prayer, through other support, but in order really to learn from our mistakes, we must suffer the consequences of our actions.

I knew a man who was very bright. He was in the entertainment industry, and he had found some success. He had also gotten interested in drugs. One day he was caught in possession of an illegal narcotic. When he stood before the judge, he had a kind of epiphany. The man realized he already knew the lesson. He wanted to say, "Judge, I get it. There is no reason to sentence me, because I have learned my lesson from this now, and I will not make those mistakes again." The judge sent him to prison anyway, of course. Although the man felt he had learned his lesson, he still needed to pay the price. His arrogance had a cost, but when he came out of prison, the lesson stayed with him.

> *It is hard to sneak a look at God's cards.*
> *But that He would choose to play dice with the world …*
> *is something I cannot believe for a single moment.*
> *—Albert Einstein*[8]

Years ago the payment for soldiers was often the privilege to rape whom they chose. Hence, a soldier raped three innocent girls on a farm and killed their parents and then, due to 'luck,' he lived out the rest of his days without ever having paid the price and died at 75 years of age. Is that justice? No. Is it balanced? No, not if you see only that picture. That is not balanced, but we know that life is. That part of the story is the pendulum swinging out. Eventually that pendulum must swing in, with just as much force. When he comes back into this world, he will receive everything that he passed out in the life or lives he had before. Perhaps he comes back as an innocent girl and suffers the same fate he provided the young farm girls. If you put these two lives together, suddenly, you have perfect balance, harmony.

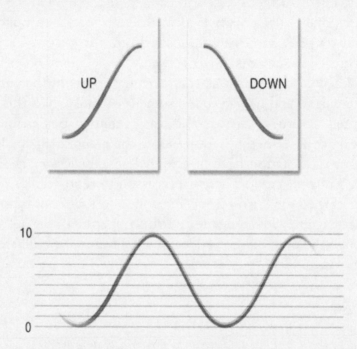

Karma is like a bell-curve. Cut the bell in half, and either side will fall over, but together the two sides are in perfect equilibrium. If you only see one side, you may never believe in the other side. If you see only the night, you will never understand daylight. But because you know the night brings the day, and the positive is proof of the negative, you must believe that harmony exists within our souls and our deeds. Like breathing, what goes in will come back out. What we sow we shall reap.

It used to be that people with afflictions were shunned because they were obviously cursed, and these curses were thought to be contagious. Karma is not contagious.

THE TEST

Now it came to pass after these things
that God tested Abraham …
(Genesis 22:1)

All man-made things are designed in theory first, and they all have one thing in common. They are tested. Food is taste-tested, drugs are lab-tested, cars are road-tested. Every product is tested and tested again before it reaches the market. The initial design theories are tested and some of them fail, generating new theories or improvements that also require testing. The average car takes a full eight years of theory-test-new-theory before it becomes a car ready for unveiling.

Souls in front of God all want to be good and beautiful and wonderful, brave and righteous. God says something like, "Okay. I'll set you up to see what you are made of." And so the testing begins, and with it, the product is bettered.

There once were two close friends who decided to go into business together. They started a restaurant that became quite successful. Joe ran the books, because numbers and accounting were his strength, and Tom took care of the front: design, advertising, and hiring staff. These two gentlemen had been buddies for so long Tom would swear on his mother's soul that Joe would never cheat him. Joe would say the same thing about Tom. The only problem was that one of them was wrong. While it was true that Joe had remained faithful to the friendship throughout decades, he could not be trusted when the temptation proved too alluring. Joe was completely honest until he realized he could cheat. He had the code to the safe, and Tom was too busy with the front to check up on him. Slowly and methodically, Joe stole all the money from the safe, and told Tom that although business appeared to be booming out front, the restaurant was faltering. He shrugged his shoulders, reporting that bank deposits were minimal and not enough to cover expenses. Tom went to work harder than ever to attract customers and oversee proper management of the restaurant, never suspecting the betrayal, but Joe was only working harder in the back to siphon off the money. Eventually, the restaurant closed, and they both lost the business. Joe was a wealthy man by that point, but Tom was destitute.

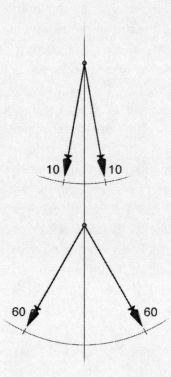

Both Tom and Joe were tested.

Joe was tested when Tom trusted him with the money and with the code to the safe. With so much at stake, he chose money over loyalty, self over love. It is a miserable test to fail, because once you fail that, the road back is very difficult. Joe had never intended to screw Tom, who was his best friend, but he failed the test when it came.

Tom was tested by the betrayal. This is a test. What would his reaction be? Forsaking their friendship, Joe goaded Tom, saying Tom would never find him, and he went to live on an island far away. Tom knew it would be easy to track Joe down and do violent things to him, which is what he wanted to do. Every night when he went to bed, he devised a different plan of exacting his revenge, and every morning, upon waking, he brooded about all the things he missed from his life because of Joe's treachery. He also knew it was well within his character to follow through on all his evil imaginings. This was the test: act upon his musings or heed the teachings of Christ and forgive?

Tom suffered with all the anger and hatred in his chest. It was certainly challenging to follow the message of Christ. But pragmatically, Tom only hurt himself with the loathing he harbored. While it may have been easier to slip into that pity party and even travel to where Joe had holed up to exact his revenge, Tom chose the more difficult, but ultimately soul-bettering option and opened his heart. Tom needed to reach deep inside himself to convert hatred into love and forgiveness. That was a test he passed.

Is it generosity if it is easy?

Jack knows that he is a very generous man. Give him a brother, Al, and a million dollars. He loves his brother, who asks him for $10, and naturally Jack gives him the $10, as he has plenty to spare. Change the scene and Jack now has only half a million dollars, and Al now needs $10,000. That is still no problem for Jack, because he loves his brother and still can spare the money. Neither of these two scenarios are actual tests, because the answers are too easy. Scene three has Jack with $100,000, and through some strange circumstances Al now desperately needs $50,000. Jack needs his $100,000, but he is conflicted over his brother's need. Is this a test? Yes, three is a true test. In scene four, Jack has $10,000 and Al needs $12,000. What does Jack do?

The first two scenarios are not really interesting because, through love, Jack would do that which is easy for him. But as the situation changes, it becomes more and more difficult for Jack to step up, and fewer people would behave in a loving manner toward their own brothers, given those criteria. In the final scenario, most of us would fail in Jack's shoes.

But there are people in the world who would not fail that test. Mother Teresa, for instance, gave up everything she owned for the rest of her life. She sacrificed not for someone close to her. She devoted her entire life to total strangers.

We are all being tested every day.

Small tests and big. Imagine if nothing you do in life is lost; everything is recorded for eternity. Every action is a response to each test you are given. Would you want to see that report card?

Most of the situations you are given in this world are tests. Even if it is karmic for you, it is most likely also a test. Once you start to view the world's trials this way, that broader perspective will help you escape the trap of self-pity, so you can move on to the greater task of crafting your soul. Tests are opportunities for spiritual growth, which is why you are on earth.

> *I know God will not give me anything I can't handle.*
> *I just wish that He didn't trust me so much.*
> *—Mother Teresa*

CARRYING THE WEIGHT OF OTHERS

One of the principles of life is the overcoming of resistance (tests), like weight training in a gym. Our responses to resistance are what define us. I can also take weight upon me: that of my spouse, my brother, or my close friend with cancer. Christ died on the cross not because he was bad; completely to the contrary, of course. Christ died on the cross because he took the weight of mankind's sins upon himself.

> *The vast universal suffering feel as thine:*
> *Thou must bear the sorrow that thou claimst to heal;*
> *The day-bringer must walk in darkest night.*
> *He who would save the world must share its pain.*
> *If he knows not grief, how shall he find grief's cure?*
> *—Sri Aurobindo*[9]

We can each do the same thing. Of course, when we see a loved one struggling under the tremendous strain of their own test, most of us would rush to his aide. That is what carrying the weight of others means. When given the opportunity to shoulder someone else's burden, it is another test for your soul. If I take my dear, frail mother to the airport and I get out of my car and carry her luggage to the check-in, it is my choice, to carry her baggage (resistance). My help is born of love and so I gladly take her weight upon me. There is a spiritual side of this phenomenon, which is not easily imagined in concrete terms. Suppose you have a dear friend who is in trouble. Perhaps they have done something wrong and are paying for it. You really love this person and it pains you to see them struggling, so you proclaim your wish to help them. Through prayer and through your own pain over their hardship, you shoulder some of their burden. In essence, you may be carrying someone else's weight in this life and not even know it.

For this reason, we cannot judge that someone is bad simply because they are straining under a heavy load, even though, often enough, our problems stem from our own actions.

At some point one may start to wonder, "why am I so lucky that I sit in my comfy chair while hundreds of thousands of people are starving in Ethiopia?" This is a valid question if you look at it only from the plane of your own experience.

Back to school.

A student in high school who is about to graduate asks, "Why do I get to graduate while there are so many students here in ninth, tenth or eleventh grades who will not graduate now?" Those other students do not have the course experience that the graduating student has, and there is a hierarchy to school and graduation, just as there is a hierarchy to awakening.

We come from a world of gases, to cells, to a world of animals and then humans, and then, out of the human world, we began to awaken spiritually and become more and more evolved. Some flowers bloom in spring and some in summer, and there is a schedule to their bloom time, just as it is with spirituality for human beings. Some people have already evolved into a higher spiritual form, and some yet have a long awakening process to work through. Eventually you will be pure spirit.

So when you ask why some people are suffering and others are not, you cannot have the answer unless you can see the entire picture, and understand all the variables. Some students are too young. Some have not studied all they need. Some students failed their tests too often and will not graduate. Let it be enough to know that we all have our own paths.

This world faces resistance and by its resistance, it grows stronger. Souls are here in abundance. By struggling and learning here in this world, we become stronger and truer and more God-like. And by helping those who struggle beside us we actually help ourselves. By passing out good in this world, good returns to us.

Someone else's struggles are an opportunity for our own goodness, to pay it forward.

We gain nothing by trying to judge others' suffering, for that story is but a paragraph in an epic that we are not privileged to read. An innocent baby that dies at three months of age proves nothing more than that we are missing most of the pages. We cannot see the bigger picture, but must trust that there is one.

The proof of that is in the laws that make up the universe.

John suffers from terrible back pain, but his life has been picture-perfect. He cannot understand why he suffers so much, after leading a fully righteous, loving life. Perhaps he comes to the conclusion that this suffering is payment for an old debt from a previous existence. What can John possibly do about it now? Take the example of putting on weight. A man has put on 45 pounds over the years, by overeating and overindulging. He cannot alter that in one day, of course, but today he can certainly decide to make a change in his ways, to eat less and exercise. Over time, he will eventually lose that extra weight, if he is diligent and dedicated. He will be changed five months or a year from now. He cannot undo the mistakes he made and regurgitate the pasta and the bread, but he can, going forward, modify their effects.

If you have done things that precipitated karmic suffering in your life, you cannot have a do-over or take back anything that has transpired. But, going forward, you can make the decision to do better, to make up for the past. The test is in how you handle the here and now. You can pay your debt confident that although the reason is elusive, it exists, and your triumph will elevate you in the end. You can go to church, repent for any sins, and show God and the universe and yourself that from now on you will be a different and better individual than before.

God does not throw dice.

You do not get run over by a car by chance. The plum does not fall from the tree by accident. It falls from the tree when it is ripe, within its quantity of time. Pick it too early, and it is green. Too late, and it rots on the ground. Everything has its own quality of time, in an assigned quantity of time. Often when people suffer tragedy they will say afterward, "I wouldn't trade it for the world—it's made me a better person." They never would have wished for the problems they had, but having those challenges changed them for the better. Knowing that life is not filled with chance makes that paradigm shift easier. Knowing that everything happens for a reason will give you the impetus to roll up your sleeves and get the most out of unpleasant situations. That is certainly a more reasonable way to deal with adversity than to sit around moaning about it not being fair. Since life is ultimately fair, jump in and do your best to improve yours and the lives of others.

Pragmatically, suffering exists because without it we could never know joy. The law of polarity requires one for the other to be experienced. In that context, who are we to question the suffering in this world? We are only here to accept it and try to diminish it to the best of our abilities.

> *Never to suffer would never to have*
> *been blessed.*
> *—Edgar Allen Poe*

Chapter 11

Is Life Predestined
or Do I Have Free Choice?

It is not in the stars to hold our destiny but in ourselves.
—William Shakespeare

Cosmos is the Greek word for order. In the cosmos' cosmos, the order of the universe, we find all our answers.

Destiny or choice? These two concepts seem diametrically opposed, so you might reasonably assume it is an either/or proposition. It is not. They are not opposites, or even mutually exclusive.

Life is BOTH predestined and free choice.

What is life? Is life day or night, good or bad, plus or minus, hot or cold?

It is both, in sequence. Polarity is in everything. Life is both summer and winter, where one follows the other. Life is successively good and evil, and so we have free choice and also predestination, in sequence.

Your choices form your destiny.

Here is how it works. You willingly decide to work out at the gym for an hour. That is free choice. By making that choice, you have destined your muscles to grow by that much. Basically, you are creating your karma as you go through this life, by everything that you do or say or even think. At the same time, you are receiving the karma that is due you as you plan and breathe. Your free choice has created and continues to create your destiny. Whatever happens to you now is part of this cycle. It is a big circle, and everything is part of this big revolving ring.

All of your choices effectuate by-products and results. You can choose to lie to people, and when they find out they will dislike you for it. It was your choice to lie, but once you lied, the outcome was predetermined. It is possible the person you lied to might never find out, but still your lie is there for all eternity, and its effects, even if not materialized in this lifetime, exist within your soul. The universe records all of your choices, not in a material manner, but in a spiritual fashion. By doing, by pushing, by deciding, by thinking, by saying, and by choosing, even if choosing to be still, you resolutely create the shape of your soul. The year 2009 built entirely upon the year 2008, which would not have existed unless preceded by 2007.

> *God will not suffer man to have a knowledge of things to come;*
> *for if he had prescience of his prosperity, he would be careless;*
> *and if understanding of his adversity,*
> *he would be despairing and senseless.*
> *—Saint Augustine*

You want to go to university. You will not get there by becoming the high school druggie/drop out. If you find school too challenging, you have no support at home, and life is too tough, perhaps you will neglect your studies and start into drugs. That road leads very shortly to the streets, or maybe you will get a job making change at the video store. Your choice to forego graduating high school predestined you away from university, away from getting a well paid job, having a family. The good news is that because of free choice you can also affect that destiny. And so, at 27, once you realize your mistakes with drugs and skipping school, you get clean and enter into a GED program. You go to college where you meet your spouse, and turn your life around. It is all possible. That was probably an even harder road, but it was the one you chose, and so it was 'meant to be.'

Whatever we pass out at any time will come back to us eventually. It looks like a stroke of unfairness, the freak accident that took a finger, but God does not play dice. The accident was caused by something, or some action. It was preceded by some essence, and it portends some lesson. It is unimportant from where the ordeal derives as long as the lesson is learned. And the lessons are always the same: grace, love, and forgiveness.

All the trials we have in this life are tests of our fortitude and our attitude.

If I push a pendulum out, yes, it will take its time to return to its original position, and then go in the opposite direction equally. If I take one or two or three pictures after a millisecond, I see the pendulum suspended in motion. If I watch it for only a moment I cannot appreciate its entire path. But it does have an entire cycle, not just a half-cycle. Give it its quality of time and it will come back. Pendulums are not instantaneous, but they are predictable.

> *We who lived in concentration camps can remember the men*
> *who walked through the huts comforting others, giving away*
> *their last piece of bread. They may have been few in number,*
> *but they offer sufficient proof that everything can be taken*
> *from a man but one thing: the last of the human freedoms—*
> *to choose one's attitude in any given set of circumstances."*
> *—Victor Frankl*

If you have troubles, there are three possibilities for their metaphysical source, and we discuss those in the chapter on suffering. Suffice it to say that for the most part, either you or God designs the challenges you face in order to improve your soul. For the purposes of this chapter, we will discuss karmic problems, what you passed out, either in this lifetime or one before. You receive exactly what you have wrought; and acceptance, overcoming and doing better is the call to action.

There is a fire that rages through a canyon in Southern California, and it devastates several homes. They are each burned to a crisp. Yet, in the middle of this, there are twelve homes that miraculously remain completely untouched. It makes no sense on the face of it, because the fire passed not ten feet from those houses, but they endured unscathed. It seems unfair! These people's homes were spared while others suffered immeasurable loss, but the fact is it was not their time. This would not be their mountain to climb. What did the others do to deserve this tragedy? If karma played a part in this ordeal, then a definitive answer is elusive, but it exists. Perhaps not in this life, maybe a thousand years ago. To karma, it makes no difference, as time is irrelevant. But they are reaping today what they sowed at some point.

This is in no way a call to judgment. None of us are without sin or our own karma. Because karma may come in any lifetime but we are materialistic in this lifetime, our judgment is ill-placed here. We should not look at someone who has cancer and presume that they brought it on themselves. Perhaps at some point in the sea of time their soul's persona did something that has manifested as cancer in the here and now, but the person we know today may not have actually perpetrated the deed that bore this result. In other words, because our judgment in this regard can only contemplate the current time, it cannot account for potentially karmic events such as cancer, or fires, or things that do not even appear to us as free choice.

We know on a mystical level that cause and effect is always in play, but on a substantial level we must admit that we are all fighting these battles in order to grow our souls into more beautiful beings. Why did the fire not destroy those other twelve homes? They were "lucky" this time.

You are in control of your destiny, through your thoughts and actions.

Although much of this life seems out of your control, you have abundant free choice all the time. Your options always include your perspective, your emotions, and your reactions. Life will offer challenges. If it never did, it would not be worth living. Your response to the gauntlet life throws down in front of you is how you shape your soul, craft your character, and also how you *choose* your destiny.

Choice governs destiny.

Chapter 12

Why Do I Need Forgiveness?

The weak can never forgive.
Forgiveness is the attribute of the strong.
—Gandhi

I have a friend, Gina. She is a pretty woman who harbors some negativity and anger, but never could understand the source of her vague frustration. She always wondered why peaceful happiness eluded her.

Then, she had a dream …

In her dream, she was in a prison as a visitor. She recognized people in the prison cells: specifically her mother, father and husband. There were more people, but those were the ones she was focused on in the dream. She wanted to leave the prison, and turned toward the door only to find it was closed. Suddenly, right in front of her stood Jesus Christ, blocking her way out. He quietly pointed to her hand. She looked down and found a key in her open hand. She slowly looked around the prison and saw that her key would fit all the locks of the prison. She understood from this, even inside the dream, that she alone held the power to release those people into forgiveness, and that until she did, she too would be like a prisoner in the jail for as long as she held that key.

Her own sobs woke her with a start. Tears streamed down her face. She did not get back to sleep that night.

The next morning she phoned her mother to apologize for the anger and resentment that she had harbored for well over a decade. She had silently reproached her parents for the limitations placed on her growing up. The tears flowed as she released all the wasted emotions over battles fought long ago. Her mother cried, also, finally learning about the issues that had kept her daughter at an indefinable distance for all these years. Together they celebrated the newfound closeness of their relationship with relief and joy. Gina has discovered, through forgiveness, a durable happiness.

> *To forgive is to set a prisoner free*
> *and discover that the prisoner was you.*
> —*Lewis B. Smedes*

Forgiveness is difficult. It may seem a lot easier to carry a grudge, but that bitterness is heavier than you think. Imagine all the energy you have spent feeling justifiably hurt and frustrated at being mistreated by someone, either purposefully or accidentally; all that emotion and stress, directed toward someone who does not even feel it. You might think they know you are angry or upset, or unforgiving, but if they felt any remorse for what they had done, they would feel that *regardless* of your emotions, once you made the insult apparent. If they are not willing to make reparations, to apologize or repay you, your emotional contribution is no longer relevant.

You cannot will someone into action by withholding forgiveness.

Why hold a grudge, then? The main reason we hold grudges is because we feel entitled, and entitlement masquerades as power.

Someone hurt me and now I get my turn to hurt them back, to show them how it feels, or I will wish bad things for them. While all this "eye for an eye" passion is understandable, it is ridiculously illogical and terribly unhealthy. Your thoughts create your world. While you are thinking evil thoughts, your world becomes that malevolence. You are graciously inviting evil into your life even though you may be wishing it on someone else, because you only have power over your own world, not anyone else's.

Consider Gina again. When she was a teenager, her parents had refused to let her attend a specialized school in New York, although she had been accepted. She bitterly regrets not going and feels it would have bettered her life immeasurably. Her parents had been justifiably afraid for her safety. For fifteen years an unyielding mood of betrayal and loss haunted Gina's ongoing relationship with her mother, whom she deeply loved. She could not see her way to forgiveness, and did not understand it until her dream. Compounding that, Gina's mother was unaware of the trouble, and could not envision anything specific to ask her daughter since the issue had begun so long ago. Not realizing there was anything to apologize for, Gina's mother essentially betrayed Gina a second time. (At least, Gina *felt* that way.) Unfortunately, Gina's perspective was still that of the fifteen-year-old girl who could not live her dream. If she could have changed that viewpoint, and realized the dangers to a fifteen-year-old on the streets of New York, it might have colored her reaction. For instance, the story could just as easily be about a young girl who went to New York and got raped in the subway, and never forgave her parents for agreeing to send a sheltered young teenager to fend for herself in a big city. But that is not this story, and Gina was too focused on the perceived injustice of being denied the New York experience. For fifteen years, Gina carried this chip on her shoulder, *even though she was the only one who knew!*

She had effectively locked her mother in a jail cell of blame, but Mom did not know, which frustrated Gina even more.

To what end? The anger and bitterness colored only Gina's world.

Forgiveness will never change the past, but it can vastly improve the future.

Bob decided he did not want to be married to her any longer. He fought a lot with his wife, Marcy, so they resolved to have a trial separation for a few months, and see if they could mend the damage they had already done to their relationship. Bob started dating right away, having no intention of repairing anything. As far as he was concerned, it was too broken to fix.

It had taken a lot of work to get to an agreement on the separation, but Marcy knew it was the right thing to do. Still, she could not deny her anger towards Bob and his uncaring ways. Did he feel her pain? Perhaps he did, but he was mainly caught up in his own pain, and, in fact, her pain was what he was escaping. The more pain she threw toward him, the faster he ran. This is a fascinating dichotomy. Her unforgiving attitude strove to keep him close, to control him; but it was actually driving him away. Bob moved to another town, set up a new home, and basically "got on with his life." Marcy, however, held onto her grudge. She locked him into a cell in the "forgiveness prison" in her mind, and there kept them both captive.

The grudge was what she knew and what made her comfortable. Resentment is often what we cling to, because it is naturally tied to our pride, and pride makes us feel whole again after an injury. We wish the other person ill so that it will all be even in the end. "He'll get his. He deserves it." The interesting thing is, though, that while you are wishing your enemies ill, the better part of you is censoring yourself, condemning yourself for those bad thoughts. You feel bad for harboring evil thoughts about someone else, no matter what they have done to you. You find yourself justifying those curses. You feel dirty asking for what is fair. Vindication is powerful, but its power is evil, and it brings evil to you.

True power is found in the choice to let something go.

EXTERNAL FORGIVENESS

Forgiveness does not require continuing the relationship.

Forgiveness can take two forms, internal and external. If someone comes to you, contritely asking for your forgiveness, and they are truly repentant for whatever insults that they have thrown your way, be gracious and accept their apology. Perhaps they have changed, perhaps this is their pattern of behavior and they will do it again. What you do with the relationship after they have made their amends is entirely up to you. Once you have accepted their apology, you are quit, released from any obligation. You owe them nothing. That is external forgiveness.

> *Forgiveness is the fragrance that the violet sheds*
> *on the heel that has crushed it.*
> *—Mark Twain*

Two women, Janet and Tracy, are close friends who go into the jewelry business together. Collectively, they host successful jewelry parties and begin to make a steady income. Janet is happy to continue in concert, but Tracy figures that if she can rid herself of Janet and hire a part-time employee to handle the trivial tasks, she will keep more profit for herself. Tracy starts to spread nasty rumors about Janet, and eventually uses them to distance herself from Janet and take over the business. Why would she betray her good friend in this way? Greed, selfishness, stupidity? (Pick one.)

Internal forgiveness requires no effort on the part of the offender.

INTERNAL FORGIVENESS

Janet eventually puts two and two together and deduces Tracy's immense, hurtful duplicity. Forgiveness, in this instance, is a very difficult pill to swallow. How can Janet forgive the woman who had begun as a trusted friend, and yet had used and betrayed her so thoroughly?

This is how: Jesus Christ.

In Christ resides an example that is impossible to deny.

Janet spent a lot of time praying about it and dissecting it. She realized that her indignation and anger was hurting her more than Tracy. In fact, it did not even touch Tracy. If Janet could just lift that veil of bitterness her life would undoubtedly improve.

… And forgive us our trespasses,
as we forgive those who trespass against us …

In The Lord's Prayer, probably the most succinct and beautifully written statement of Christianity, this stanza is the most difficult to utter. Who among any of us holds no resentment toward another person? In these two lines Christ lays down the foundation for our own redemption. He clearly states that for us to be forgiven for our sins, in order to enter the kingdom of heaven, we must forgive all others. It is a stipulation. It is not a negotiation. The part "as we forgive" means that we *must* forgive to the same degree that we wish to be forgiven; in other words, entirely.

Forgiveness is not easy, but it is simple. Christ demands that we forgive each other because we are all offenders. All of us need forgiveness from each other. More importantly, though, is the underlying release that forgiveness gives to the giver. If we can unburden ourselves from the shackles that are our grudges, we are then, and only then, free to live loving lives.

To dwell in the pain of relational failure is to condemn yourself to misery.
To forgive is to release yourself from that same misery.

Janet knelt down one day in an empty church, and she let Tracy go. She said, "I forgive Tracy and I pray for her soul." She understood that she, herself, was not without sin. She wanted to release Tracy and the painful emotions she felt when she reflected on the sordid story of their friendship and business. Tracy had done something incomprehensible to Janet, but it no longer mattered. Janet did not need to like Tracy to forgive her. Janet simply needed to free Tracy, in order to free herself. That is internal forgiveness.

Forgiveness did not change the women's outward relationship, but it changed Janet's relationship with herself.

Tracy was on a different path. Janet wished Tracy a better life, and a better understanding of right and wrong.

Forgiveness does not demand that you like the person again.

When you forgive someone, you are not required to become best friends again. There is no need to phone them to let them know that you forgive them, unless they ask for forgiveness. Offering forgiveness to people who do not want it seems like a waste of time. Chances are, they are proceeding with their own life, oblivious to, or even rejoicing in whatever evil they managed to bring into your life. *Reject that evil.* Turn it away from your heart with a forgiving prayer, and move forward without it.

To err is human. To forgive is pragmatic.

If we want to follow Christ, to become like Christ, we must behave as he did. We should never say, "If something bad happens to me, I hope it happens to you, too." That is vengeance. The better plan is to immediately forgive them, release them (and yourself) from the burden of hatred. Christ taught us to love our neighbors, but forgive our enemies.

If someone does wrong by me, my hatred of him will not actually hurt him unless I act on it. To willfully harm him is a sin and a black gash on my soul. But what if I do not act on it? Imagine I do nothing but harbor extreme resentment toward the person. What then? The bad guy wins again. He doubles his return because of my inability to forgive! I am hurting *myself* in this way, which is also a sin. All the time I spend picturing evil things happening to my tormentor is time I deny myself enjoyment of my life. All those evil destructive thoughts I have displace any positive or constructive thoughts I might have.

Devastation in place of creation.

We are here to counter this reactive equation. We are here to release these consequences. Christ, on the cross, asked God the Father to forgive the people who delivered His undeserved punishment, explaining they did not know what they were doing. This is an extremely powerful example.

Does this mean if a friend cheats you, you should just forgive him and go play golf together? Absolutely not! But harboring resentment only hurts you, so forgive him, move on, (and stay away from him). Lesson learned. It seems much easier to hate and let it fester. This is exactly how evil wins. Evil easily begets evil. That is the challenge we all equally face.

A loving thought is already part of the way to the truth.

On the average Sunday when I go to church, there is a positive repetitive exercise about the beauty of life, respect towards others, and how to project goodness into everyday living. You should not lie. You should not steal. There is an encouraging air in church, and the more I turn to it, the more I become that fabric.

Practice makes perfect.

My father was an actor. In a stage play once he played the part of a drunken villain who was very brutal and he had to scream a lot. After a year (about 300 performances,) he told me, "You know, it's very strange, because it rubbed off on me. I have become more violent and aggressive. I am much more short-tempered because I had to slip into this part again and again, even though I knew it was just a play. But it rubbed off on me." Of course, practice makes perfect. If you scream and pretend to be nasty for a full year, you will eventually start to use that in your everyday life. It would be very difficult to fight that. Conversely, if week after week you expose yourself to the loving, embracing message of the church, you will start to use it in your life. Try to forgive people as a daily exercise, even for people who have no knowledge they need it. The distracted woman in the car ahead of you who misses the turn signal. The dry-cleaner who takes his time finding your pick-up. Forgive them as you go. Smile at them instead. If you practice forgiving, it will come easier to you. Look at past grudges and set them free. Set yourself free of them. Release the rancor in your heart and forgive yourself for clinging to those grudges for as long as you have.

Forgiveness is the currency of the soul.

Imagine you are in a sea of people, all of whom are faulty, all of whom have sinned. You stand amidst them, screaming at their shortcomings, pointing out their faults. Suddenly they all turn to stare at you, and you become transparent. Your every fault is evident for the world to see, and the people you were criticizing are now pointing at all of your iniquities. How ashamed would you be? We must learn to forgive people their faults, if only because our own are so plentiful.

Let he who is without sin cast the first stone.
(John 8:7)

Chapter 13

How Do I Find God?

Man sieht nur das, was man weiß.
We only see what we know.
—Johann Wolfgang von Goethe

Our eyes cannot perceive a computer if we do not understand the idea of the computer. We may simply assume it is a funny-looking television sitting on the desk, and then be easily distracted by something we did recognize, like the clock. You cannot know it if you cannot name it. Remember, at the beginning of this book, the 3-D pictures that I initially had trouble making sense of? If I had not known they were supposed to be viewed in 3-D, I never would have seen them that way. They would have simply been some funky computer-rendered compositions and nothing more. Because I knew what to look for, resonance allowed me to perceive it.

RESONANCE

The law of resonance refers to our inherent ability to understand or accept information or knowledge.

Resonate: \'re-zə-ˌnāt\ verb
1 : to produce or exhibit resonance
2 : to respond as if by resonance <resonate to the music>; also
  : to have a repetitive pattern that resembles resonance
3 : to relate harmoniously : strike a chord <a message that
  resonates with voters>[10]

A friend phones me and tells me to turn on Channel 20. If I have no TV, putting on Channel 20 would be impossible. Channel 20 may be broadcasting, but without resonance, or the ability to receive the information, it is useless to me.

If we go into a museum, but know nothing about art, then looking at remarkable works of art will be much less moving than if we had studied and could truly appreciate the artwork for all it represents and for its history. Knowledge deepens our appreciation and the effect of our exposure to the artwork. Many people do not enjoy opera because they never learned to appreciate it.

It's an acquired taste.

There have been studies done on babies who were blindfolded at birth. Their brains formed as normal children's brains do except for one thing: being deprived of the use of their eyes, they never developed sight. They have the tools: their eyes, optic nerves and brain tissues are all healthy, but since they were prevented from learning to "see," their brains never formed the nerve pathways, and so, although in principle they can "see," in practice they do not perceive sight. Their brains cannot understand images, and consequently they are blind.

An old black and white TV set receives a broadcast today, in color. The TV is unable to process the color information, (it doesn't resonate) so the picture on the TV is still in black and white. The information is available, but unrecognizable.

I never used to play tennis. When I would chance upon a tennis match on TV, I would simply change the channel. It held absolutely no interest for me. Then I started taking tennis lessons. The more I exposed myself to the game and its various components, the more I learned. I became more interested. Soon, when I came across a match on TV, I would sit, transfixed by it. I knew the players; I understood when someone scored a difficult shot. The game had become much more exciting for me because it resonated with the knowledge I already had. It had all become relevant to me through my exposure to, and study of, the game.

The law of resonance applies similarly in our quest to know God. Someone who absolutely denies the existence of God will have great trouble in seeing any of the sense of this book, perhaps. Conversely, someone who wants to know, and is receptive to finding God, can certainly appreciate the message of this book. It is impossible for God to reach someone who has not begun to cultivate some of the qualities of God within himself. Lucky for us, we are born with some of these characteristics (the Moral Law) and only through actively denying them can we lose them.

If you have no yearning to meet Him, if you have no desire for knowledge, if you do not want His goodness, if you refuse to cultivate these traits within you, He cannot reach you. You pass by a church and it is just another building to you. You might even walk into a church during a mass and hear the priest speak but it is empty sounds. Only if you start cultivating the language or the code of what is being projected can it reach you. The more you develop our understanding, the more relevance this language will have in your life, the more *resonance* it will find in your soul.

Our relationship with God is based on resonance.

I could be the most gifted musician but if I have no audience my gift is irrelevant to all but myself. I can create a masterpiece of a film, but without a projector, a screen and an audience, it may as well go in the dumpster. No orchestra would play to an empty hall again and again, and no audience would come to a vacant theater. One needs the other.

The music resonates with the audience and the audience's response energizes the orchestra.

They both need each other. God created man to need Him, and He needs man and yearns for the love of mankind. He gave us free choice, but still wants and desires for us to choose him. Like any parent-child relationship, the parent yearns for the child to turn to him or her, but gives the child the liberty to choose, and so to learn. The God-human relationship mimics this human-human bond that He also created. Through the law of polarity, we can assume the parallels are consistent. God wants to be unified with His children, and He longs for them to make the choice for that unity.

We have the ability to make that selection every day. Each and every day we can go to church or read the Bible to cultivate our relationship with God. It is never too late. The sooner I start, the more I will know. The deeper my knowledge grows, the more profound my hunger. Each day we may open up to this knowledge, or be distracted by any of a myriad of options. Choosing to learn more about God, to get closer to the essence of life, will yield a greater understanding of what we truly face.

I am afraid I shall not find Him, but I shall still look for Him.
If He exists, He may be appreciative of my efforts.
—Jules Renard

With more exposure to music and a greater understanding of the mechanics and nature of composition, I become more of a sophisticated aficionado and less like a casual audience member, and the symphony carries more meaning for me. A casual listener, while he may appreciate how beautiful the music is, cannot fully comprehend its incredible depth, because he is limited by his inexperience, by his incomplete study of the subject. For him, one symphony is much like any other. If he has no interest in music then it makes no difference which symphony plays. In a sense, he might as well be deaf.

There is no question for me as to the existence of God. The only question I have is why so many people are deaf and blind to Him. For many people God is but an uninteresting theory. For the seeker, the laws of the universe are undeniable, immutable proof of God. You may tell someone that there are germs on a cloth, and they will believe you because they learned in school (seen as authority) about those pesky invisible things that cause sickness. Tell the same person about God as creator, and they raise their eyebrows. They have no confidence in your authority. They respond that they cannot see God (though the same answer is true for germs). They admit they themselves exist, and yet they doubt having been created.

> *If you gain, you gain all; if you lose, you lose nothing.*
> *Wager, then, without hesitation that He exists.*
> *—Blaise Pascal*

Once I realized the nature of God and the knowledge of Him, I needed to grow in Him, sometimes to the extreme. For me, extreme meant that I would go into church each day and pray on my knees. This was typically during difficult times when I really needed His guidance and comfort. My pain propelled me to seek God like I know I never would have otherwise. I was desperate to feel the strength that comes from a supreme being, and the comfort that a greater power gives a meager one.

I knelt in church once to pray, "Jesus, please stop my suffering." The moment I spoke those words I heard a voice, as if inside my head, say, "You say you want to follow me, but only in the ways you deem right." I looked up at the Christ on the crucifix, His face distorted in pain, and suddenly I was much more accepting of my own pain. Knowing what Christ willingly endured on my behalf made my hardships pale in comparison. I made quantum leaps in my faith, in my understanding, and in my love towards God, when I was most challenged with difficulty and distress.

Struggles lead us toward God.

The times I spent sitting around on a beach or going to restaurants and parties were, of course, the times that my relationship with God began to suffer. I excelled at "God" in times when I desperately needed the relationship to strengthen me and carry me, but in easy times, when I was more self-sufficient, I stopped communicating with Him as much, and I lost the skill. To use the tennis analogy, it was as if I had been a great tennis player but stopped playing. When I took up the racket again I needed to work out some kinks in my strokes.

There is a radio receiver in South America that is the size of an enormous crater. Isn't it obvious? The larger the receiver, the better the reception. Here is a simple corollary to your relationship with God. God can be compared to an eternal radio wave, and it depends entirely on you how much you are willing to receive. If you are only minimally receptive, you will get a little bit. If you open yourself a lot, you shall receive a lot. And if you actively pursue God, well, you get the point. It is all up to you: free choice.

God is infinite. Let my cup run over.

Obviously, you should turn to God not just in times of hardship but in times when life is going well, to thank him and invite him to walk with you, have a dialog, not just once a day but constantly. You have the capacity to receive much more than you might even imagine. The wonderful thing about God is that He is full-service, 24/7. You can have a conversation with Him at any time, requiring very limited effort on your part. All He asks is your devotion and dedication, that you open your heart so that He can heal you and love you.

Belief in God does not make Him real; it makes us more.

Chapter 14

Is Jesus Christ Truly the Son of God?

Loving is not just caring deeply,
it's, above all, understanding.
—Françoise Sagan

Human beings are not designed to fully comprehend God. When you type on your computer, it is translated into binary code, an incomprehensible string of zeros and ones. You cannot possibly be expected to read it in that code form, so the computer translates it back into English or Swedish or your native language.

1001010011010110101011010100101011010101010101101001010100011111 10101001

If God chooses to speak to us, he must do so in a way that we can comprehend. He is outside of time and space, and we are limited. Obviously, it is mainly up to Him to reveal Himself to us. Think for a moment on how best He could accomplish that.

Imagine you are traveling home to see your parents after an extended trip abroad. You have heavy luggage and there is a long staircase up to the door of your parents' house. Your father sees you standing there. What does a loving father do when his child needs assistance? He comes down the stairs to help you carry your luggage up to the door, so you can join him inside. As he approaches you have a choice to make. Are you willing to hand over your suitcase to accept his help?

Jesus came to offer help and hope to the world, and rescue desiring souls from eternal separation from God.

God could have arrived as wind, a talking rat, or a burning bush, but coming to us as a man was the best way to impart his message and to show understanding. But I'm getting ahead of myself here, because first we must establish who Jesus was, apart from His divinity.

> *The whole of history is incomprehensible without Him.*
> *—Ernest Renan*

Jesus was a teacher, a leader of men, a good and loving soul, a healer, a miracle worker, and a prophet. There is no one in history that comes close to His renown. More speeches have been written about Him than Alexander the Great, Caesar, Charlemagne, Napoleon, and Washington, combined. He has done more to shape the history of our world than anyone else, by light-years. He accomplished all of this before turning 34 years old. His legacy endures under the most intense scrutiny. He is worthy of our passionate contemplation, as His enduring presence and the church He founded assures us.

Anyone who denies Jesus obviously has not fully considered His story, the most incredible tale in history. In the U.S. we have war heroes who have gone through unbelievable hardship, conquered immense fear, and overcome incredible odds. They are awarded The Congressional Medal of Honor, the highest honor in the military, and they are given appropriate accolades. They are extraordinary men and women who have earned their places in history and in the hearts of free Americans nationwide. But none of their deeds on the battlefield compare to what Jesus did, to what he endured, in peacetime, from a choice He made to fulfill His destiny.

It is absurd to think that a few simple men, from different walks of life, could conspire to invent such a character and give Him the attributes for which He is credited. How? Why would they have met, to make this plan? Remember, they didn't have the Internet back then. Historians have tried to dissect the New Testament, to discredit it, to no avail. Examining it gives us a glimpse into the lives of these men, with the small details they include in their accounts. To believe their writings are part of a grand scheme to defraud people into being good and kind to one another is much more far-fetched than to believe one incredible individual convinced all these followers, through his conduct and through miraculous acts, that He was the Son of God.

"Are you the Messiah, the Son of the Blessed One?"
"I am," said Jesus.
(Mark 14:61-62)

In Jesus' day, society was a mess. (How little things have changed!) Humans were getting it all wrong in their ultimate selfishness, most notably the temple priests, who had over 400 distinct rituals to perform every day in order to fulfill their holy duties. God sent His Son to reinterpret His intentions for our lives: love and forgiveness. Jesus came to teach us a new way to worship. Among many controversial deeds, He performed a miracle on the Sabbath, which the temple priests, who were already offended by Jesus' censure, declared to be an insult to God. In response, Jesus pointed to their own hypocrisy: they would certainly save their own ailing sheep on the Sabbath, but would value a human life less. His numerous and voluble criticisms went completely against the authority of the day, and so the powerful priests determined to dispose of him. That is part of the story of Jesus. Of course, His legacy is much more than a paragraph.

Jesus completely turned the tables. He came as a pauper, not a king: the true Son of God, adopted into the royal lineage of David. He befriended and healed the outcasts and washed the feet of even the lowest, although by right He could have demanded to be served. He pardoned the sinners and criticized the holy.

Jesus made the parameters of our interaction with our Father in Heaven absolutely clear. For believers, He redefined God and His purpose. He called Himself the Son of Man and the Son of God. The phrase "Son of" means "one of" or "equal to."

Jesus of Nazareth was the most scientific man that ever trod the globe.
He plunged beneath the material surface of things,
and found the spiritual cause.
—Mary Baker Eddy

Crucifixion was a well-understood practice of the day. It is a frighteningly horrible way to die: your arms and feet are nailed to a cross, with the weight of your body pulling on the tendons and ligaments of your limbs. You are unable to move, plus you have been beaten to a pulp, the flies are licking at your dripping blood, and you fully comprehend that your only relief will come with death. It is difficult to get your brain to actually focus on this image, isn't it? I recoil from it while I write this, as I am sure most good people do. Crucifixion actually kills by suffocation. The body's weight becomes too much to allow the lungs to expand. Terrible, isn't it?

Imagine being such an intensely controversial figure, being adored and being hated, and trying only to improve peace and understanding in the world by teaching love and forgiveness. Now also picture you are going to be crucified. Really ponder this for a moment. Jesus knew what lay ahead of him before he entered the town of Jerusalem. He predicted it several times. Worse than dying on the cross, He deliberately separated Himself from His Heavenly Father by assuming all worldly sin. This was almost too painful even for Him to bear, and so He prayed in the garden of Gethsemane, "Father, if it be your will ... take this cup from me." (Mark 14:36)

A man who was completely innocent,
[Jesus] offered himself as a sacrifice for the good of others,
including his enemies, and became the ransom of the world.
It was a perfect act.
—Gandhi

Dragging the cross up the hill to certain death, where did He find the strength? How could His legs carry even just His own weight, much less the cross He bore? These are difficult thoughts to ponder, distasteful and morbid, but they are crucial to appreciating Jesus as an incredible (and undeserved) gift of God.

Why did He bother?

He could have easily just disappeared into the hills, never to be found again. He could have agreed not to criticize the priests or teach anymore. He could have done any number of things to avoid the obvious agony of crucifixion and an early death. He could have just taken His own life. He did none of that. He knowingly and willingly sacrificed Himself.

Philosophy is the love of wisdom:
Christianity is the wisdom of love.
—Augustus William Hare and Julius Charles Hare

His act is indisputable. It is incontrovertible. It is, truthfully, incomprehensible to you and me.

Only one Jesus ...

No other founder of any religion has ever dared to make even a few of the wild assertions that Jesus made about Himself. His message of love and forgiveness is yet unparalleled in the world. It is a message of hope, from a man ostensibly with none. He knew when and how he would die. He knew He would be betrayed, and by whom. He knew what tragedy He would witness, and yet He was optimistic and joyous in humanity. Either He was a complete idiot, or He was God in human form. To attempt to identify Him simply as some great moral teacher or interesting ideologue is to betray not only His legacy, but also your own intelligence. He Himself left no room for any patronizing, reluctant acceptance.

Jesus deliberately ensured that His authenticity would be evident to anyone who properly examined all the facts about Him.

He killed Death.

If there were any one thing God could do to establish His authenticity on earth, overcoming death would fit that bill. The Resurrection proved His divinity.

1. Christ correctly predicted how He would die and that three days later He would rise again.
2. There were many witnesses to the empty tomb.
3. The disciples, who were despondent after His death, were *transformed* and *reinvigorated* when they saw Him risen again.

For Christ, the only way to lead was by example. After His resurrection, Christ spent 40 more days on earth, was witnessed by hundreds of people and held conversations and discussions until He finally left to take His place in heaven. He showed His disciples how it works, and they were convinced. So began the spread of Christianity across the Roman Empire and the world, and it continues today. If there had been no resurrection, His disheartened apostles would have had no impetus to invent one, (and to sacrifice their own lives as a result of such a lie). It can be said that His resurrection did more for Christianity than all His other acts, because it proved to all His followers that they had chosen to obey the true Son of God, and so propelled them on their incredible and daunting mission to spread the word. If Christ was not resurrected from death, it is safe to postulate that He would never have achieved the renown He has in the world.

In any case, there are no other resurrections to compare it to. There is only His, authenticated by hundreds of witnesses and recorded in the New Testament. Since it is unique in history, the odds against it seem insurmountable. It was, by all human standards, a miracle. Then again, the odds against this universe and a planet actually supporting life are equally incomprehensible, but, miracle of miracles, here we are. A miracle is simply something that we cannot explain using the physical and logical laws we understand. But if there were a spiritual explanation for something that contradicts our laws, then is it less miraculous? When a caterpillar turns into a butterfly, we call that metamorphosis, which actually is a euphemism for "miracle that we accept because we witness it so often." It is all magic, until you know the trick. He is just another Man, until you know Him as God.

What is Jesus' role in our lives today? He fills the gap between God and us. When you get your bank statement every month, you reconcile it with your own bookkeeping, to make sure that you and the bank have the same numbers. Jesus reconciles your account with God. He stands for forgiveness. He set the perfect example by forgiving His tormentors as He was dying on the cross.

Father forgive them,
for they know not what they do.
(Luke 23:34)

As Jesus, God has descended to earth to help you up those stairs, to carry your luggage, and we all have an enormous amount of baggage. You cannot get up to the door to be reunited with God on your own. You have a decision to make, whether or not to accept His help in the form of Jesus. This acceptance must be made on several levels, including in your heart, your actions and your words.

Jesus Christ. When you care enough to send the very best.

Jesus showed us how to live on earth and live eternally. He is our direct line to God The Father. We pray to Him because as Man and God, having led an earthly life, and having known pain and tragedy, He understands. He taught love and forgiveness in lieu of vengeance and selfishness. He criticized the holiest priests for their judgmental marginalization of many of God's children, and he embraced sinners. For these things he was put to death.

And then He rose again on the third day.
And so the story begins …

Chapter 15

What Is Grace and Why Do I Need It?

[God] hath made him to be sin for us,
who knew no sin, that we might be made
the righteousness of God in him.
(2 Corinthians. 5:21)

Much has been written and said about the *Grace of God*. The concept of God's grace is simple, but challenging, because the grace of God is based on love, and who really understands love?

There is a drop of water.
There is a pond.
There is an ocean.

They are all water. The substance is the same in each but the dimensions change as we progress from water drop to pond, to ocean. The same principle applies abstractly to love. As human beings, most of us have experienced love at some stage, be it toward our parents, other family members, friends and so on. We know what it is like to love, yet the emotion we call love is a mere drop of water, compared to the ocean that is the love of God. We do not have the capacity to love in the same dimensions as God's love. That is why the concept of grace is so challenging.

Have you ever loved someone who hurt you? You love them anyway. True love is not meritorious. It covers faults with acceptance. When something is broken, grace says it is still loveable.

Everything that exists, everything you feel and see around you, happens only by the grace of God. Think about it! Why are there trees, and flowers, and bees, and birds? Why are there endless possibilities on this earth? Why is there even an earth to begin with? God created this opportunity for you to return to Him through an accumulation of your own decisions. With free choice in all your daily decisions, either for or against God, you are preparing your way for eternity, for your soul's entry into the place we call heaven.

God's love prepares everything so we may find our path to him.

If you love your child, or your wife, your husband, your parents, you will not do them any harm. Love is the shield against evil, against darkness, but darkness is a decision we can make as well. It does not just happen to us; we create evil in our lives. We can choose to be blinded to the offering of God's grace, which means that we choose to walk in darkness, separating ourselves from the Kingdom of Heaven. In order to enter heaven, unity with God, all darkness must be purged (by God's *grace*) from within ourselves.

Grace, in a word, means Christ's act of sacrifice on our behalf.

With His crucifixion, Christ paid for our sins, our entry fee into heaven. Alone, we can never be perfect, but with grace we may still be freed. Grace is given to all who by their own free will accept it. If we were to create a chart of several different individuals, and show their relative levels of virtue, it might look something like this:

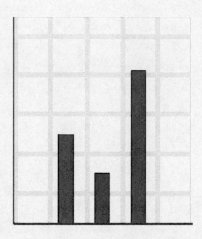

The first person goes to church sometimes, is nasty to his secretary, and he is outwardly envious of other people's success. The second person is a thief and has spent time in prison. The third person is devout and works diligently at the homeless shelter. All of them choose to follow Christ and ask for His Forgiveness. Now picture grace. Grace comes to this graph and covers it entirely.

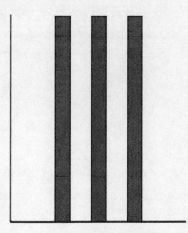

Grace is not apportioned according to who deserves it more. We all need grace equally, and in entirety. None of us can ever be "good enough," but grace can make us so. The price of our sins—all of our sins without regard to severity—has been paid for by the crucifixion and our acceptance of Christ.

As far as the east is from the west, so far has He removed
our transgressions from us.
(Psalm 103:12)

"As far as the east is from the west." That is a very long way. In fact, it is infinitely far. It does not say 'as far as north is from south,' because the two poles serve as boundaries, making it a finite distance. Once at the top, you can only go back down. But where on earth does east stop and turn back into west?

His forgiveness is unlimited.

Heaven is the timeless unification of all souls into one. God's gift allows us to enter this earth, which he created for us with the purpose of shaping our souls, like a school is created for children with the intention to shape their minds. No child is perfect in school. Some will graduate with honors and some may barely pass. Even the slacker with straight D's gets his diploma, in the end. The same applies to this life.

Grace built the school.

In school, you can graduate by fulfilling all the requirements and performing in all the tests and exams in a satisfactory manner. You do not need perfection. In the school of life, your diploma is awarded by the grace of God. It is not awarded with any regard to merit, because your merit will never be enough. A young girl practices the violin for years, making mistakes and learning from them until she is nearly perfect. Then she is accepted into the orchestra, because although she still makes some mistakes, the orchestral director considers her accomplished enough. That acceptance is like grace. Her mistakes are washed away, and she becomes seemingly perfect, in the body of the orchestra where all instruments play as one.

You cannot merit Grace.

The process of the school of life is not distinguished by time, however, but rather by the principles of karma and of purity. We strive to attain a higher level of purity, characterized by awakening out of our animalistic body into a more spiritual body. We become more spirit than flesh. This happens after yearning to be with God, after expressly wishing to be with Him, united in His love. Only then can the grace of God build a bridge for us and it is only by walking across this bridge that we can enter into heaven. Without the bridge, no matter how pure we may become, there is no way for us to enter heaven because purity in this life is completely different from purity in heaven.

Grace will build the bridge.

Picture God, standing on the opposite side of a raging river. The river is miles across, but we all want to get across, because of our innate desire to be united with our creator. Some of us are good swimmers, but this river is bigger and more treacherous than the English Channel. While one person might swim most of the way across, someone else will only swim a few feet before being swept away. Others still will stand on the shore, too afraid to dive in. Grace is a bridge that carries all of us from one shore to the other without even our feet getting wet.

Amazing Grace (how sweet the sound)
That saved a wretch like me
I once was lost, but now am found
Was blind but now I see
—John Newton

John Newton, the slave trader who was reformed and born-again, captures the essence of grace in this famous song. It is truly through grace alone that we have any hope for ourselves. If you have ever harbored one bad thought in your mind, that is impurity. That is enough to bar you from entering Heaven, where only goodness and love exist. What trumps your impurity is *grace*. Jesus came and offered Himself to pay for those sins that would otherwise prevent your ascension toward God. So the only way you can be truly forgiven and cleansed of your sins is by accepting Christ and emulating Him to the best of your abilities, and by accepting His offer that He died for your sins. Without that, you would have on your soul the refuse of all your bad deeds and sins, with no way to wash them clean. Through Christ you are awarded a clean slate, but only if you ask for it.

T'was Grace that taught my heart to fear.
And Grace, my fears relieved.
How precious did that Grace appear
The hour I first believed.
—John Newton

At the pearly gates, you look down at your clothes and see that you are dressed in tattered and soiled garments. The sins of your days on earth are visible in the ratty old clothes you wear. You cannot go through the gates in this way. You are embarrassed and ashamed by the visibility of your wretched thoughts and deeds. Then Christ appears and assures you that because you have accepted Him and followed Him, you are renewed. He washes away all the sins of your past. Christ's grace transforms you. Your tattered garments are refreshed and become clean, white linen again, simply by His profession of love and His gift of grace.

Take up your cross and follow me.
(Mark 8:34)

We each have our own burdens, and Christ's admonishment was for you to bear yours as He did His. He did not mean that the only way to achieve a state of divine grace is through immense suffering. He wants you to take this life upon yourself and follow Him. Emulate Him. Live this life fully and do not hide from it. Embrace this life with all its wonderful moments and its painful moments, too.

In contrast, see what His offer of Grace cost Him: the torture, suffering and dying on the cross. Is there really a comparison? Christ made the offer of grace in advance of any of our sins, such that we could understand the nature of that offer. It is unconditional and comprehensive. Having chosen to follow the path toward God, we may be at peace, grateful for the knowledge that God's grace will see us safely across the bridge. Our devotion brings us to the river; God's grace brings us across it and into the kingdom of heaven.

The only thing necessary for evil to flourish is for good men to do nothing.
–Edmund Burke

Sitting around doing nothing can be equated with doing evil. Wanting is not the same as creating. You can yearn all you like, but if you do not live a life dedicated to following Him, you cannot reach God.

I cannot fly to New York unless I first decide that I want to go to New York. Then I must book a ticket and I go to the airport and get on the plane. When I finally arrive in New York, it is by a string of thoughts and actions, not by chance. It is not good enough to decide to follow Christ, or to want God in your life. You have to book the ticket and go to the airport. Even then, you have to choose the right plane, or you may end up in Wichita instead of New York. If you make a decision, and then follow it with the wrong choices, do not be surprised that you are not united with God at the end of the journey. Also, not going to the airport will not get you to New York.

God gave you a physical body for a reason. He wants you to go out into the world and live by his word and also spread his cause: forgiveness. If, for instance, you sit there and say, "If I could change anything about this world then I would feed the poor," get up on your feet and feed them. You may not be able to feed all of them but you can feed some. You can reach them with your food, and your kind words, and you can make a difference. So go and make your mark. Open your mouth and activate your hands. There are many who claim to be good by virtue of never having done anything bad. That is not nearly enough. Only good acts make a person good.

Nothing comes from nothing.

An absence of action breeds further inaction. This applies to your business life, to your personal relationships, to you being a couch potato, and even to your relationship with God. Faith is not a passive thing. For faith to be effective, it needs to be a faith that is lived daily, actively. This does not mean you have to go out and seek a place in the world where you may be killed for your faith, because not everyone is called to be a martyr. Where I am living now, in Long Island, we have tulips that flower in March and early April. We also have the Montauk daisies that bloom at the end of September or early October. Is the daisy worth less than the tulip? Is a flower that blooms in April better or worse than a flower that blossoms in October? Neither, they are merely different on account of their *quality of time*.

According to the quality of time, each one of us has different lessons to learn at different stages of our lives and various lifetimes. Maturing gradually in our spirit, we reach higher stages of understanding. Stage by stage, the state of mind adjusts to the complexity of the lessons that need to be learned and understood. Thus, your lessons and my lessons, and even our country's lessons, are all independent though they may be interrelated. Eventually we will learn all the lessons that are needed to reach the eternal state of heaven. Then the Divine Conductor *grace*fully accepts us into the orchestra, and we play as one.

Grace is blessing someone even though they do not deserve it.

Grace is like the step beyond forgiveness, and we are called to grace our fellow travelers, much as we wish to have grace shed on us. Like forgiving, this is not easy to practice, but if you extend grace, more will come back to you.

A spiritual Grand Canyon condemns us to be apart from God.
It is our acceptance of Grace that bridges that vast chasm.

Like an unopened birthday gift, God's grace is there for the taking but no one will force you to grasp it. If you do not know it is your birthday, you may think that the gift is meant for someone else. It is not. Go ahead and open it. It will change your life!

> Only God's Grace has given you life,
> And Grace affords you the learning,
> Grace lifts you easily up into heaven,
> Rewarding, regardless of earning.

Chapter 16

How Can I Find Happiness?

We tend to forget that happiness doesn't come as a result
of getting something we don't have, but rather of
recognizing and appreciating what we do have.
—Frederick Keonig

Happiness has two main ingredients, neither of which is money, strangely enough! First, you must decide to be happy, and second, you must have hope for the future. Without both of these, happiness is like a tissue in a snowstorm.

CHOICE

Most folks are about as happy as they make up their minds to be.
—Abraham Lincoln

Virtually any belief is a specific choice that you make. You can rationally sit and listen to each side of the debate, but it is your choice alone which way you want to believe. For instance, "You have lost $35,000," could be good news or bad, depending on your point of view. If your savings was worth $100,000, and the market dropped, making it worth only $65,000 this news is disastrous.

But when you find out your neighbor lost his job and his $100,000 savings account was completely wiped out, the $35,000 seems small in comparison. In actuality, it is all in your head. There is another side, a worse side, to every story, so if you despair of something, look for the other side, and look at how your story is the silver lining in the cloud. That is your choice.

There is no happiness;
there are only moments of happiness.
—Spanish proverb

Two photographers fly to Paris for three days. They each photograph the city for an album. One of them goes to all the beautiful sites: the Eiffel Tower, Montmartre, L'Arc de Triumph. He takes photos of the wonderful cafes and shops, and even goes to Versailles to photograph the castle. The other photographer finds the seedy parts of the city and photographs the indigents, the prostitutes and the sewage backed up in the street. For him, the crucial location to shoot was the prison with all the dangerous, desperate prisoners. When the two photographers board the plane back home to the States, they compare albums. One of them saw a disgusting city and the other a beautiful one, just by making simple decisions of direction. For each of them, Paris signifies a completely different reality. But Paris is Paris. It is comprised of everything, good and bad. The city does not change, but each individual's experience of the city will, by his own free choice.

The film of your life is like that. Depending on what you expose it to, your soul takes on varying impressions that stay with you for a long time. The simple truth is that you become what you think, not just over one lifetime but over many, and you can decide almost anything in your mind and become it. Consequently, you must be considerate of what you think.

Your mind only goes where your desire takes it.

If you take a camera to Paris and photograph only the detritus in the streets, well, you will remember Paris as a filthy place with no beauty. But I know Paris as the city of lights, with fantastic, historical architecture. In my mind, I photographed the beauty surrounding me when I was there, and those images fill my thoughts when I hear the word Paris. This was my choice.

I felt sorry for myself because I had no shoes,
until I met a man who had no feet.
—Jewish Folk Saying

Free will aims our focus on different life experiences and imprints our souls accordingly

You stand in front of a white canvas each and every day. This is your painting, yours alone. You may now apply any and all colors on this canvas, as you wish. Do not blame anyone else, and certainly not God, for using only dark and threatening colors. Choose the bright colors and your canvas *will* be bright. Duh.

RESPONSIBILITY

The idea that you truly control your emotions is simultaneously uplifting and oppressive. Control is something we organically crave, but it also provokes a great deal of fear, because responsibility accompanies that power. Life seems "easier" without responsibility.

You are responsible for your own happiness.

Do you believe that other forces control your emotions? That, too, is your choice, but you are giving away your power. The blame game helps in avoiding responsibility and culpability, but it does not serve you. Assuming control is better. Often enough, situations or circumstances out of your control seem to dictate the way you feel, but ultimately, underneath, you decide how you react to events, not the other way round. Taking the wheel may be difficult, but in the end you finish closer to where you want to be if you get to drive that car.

Your brain absorbs the knowledge that comes to you every day through your senses. It filters this information and processes it in a sort of prism, assigning value to it as it comes in and as it is reconsidered. What may have a negative value, initially, like news that your foot is gone, can be reassigned a value when you learn they nearly took the entire leg.

If you cannot change your circumstances, adjust your perspective.

My friend likes to golf, but he is afraid of sand traps and water. He approaches water and says, "Uh oh ... I guess I'll be going swimming today!" Needless to say, his ball goes in the water 99 percent of the time. I saw this and wanted to try a little experiment for my own game. I am not a gifted golfer, and I was terrible out of sand traps. So, every time my ball went into a sand trap, I said out loud, "I am awesome out of the sand!" It made people laugh, and I laughed along with them, too. Just saying it, of course, put me in a more jovial mood than saying, "Oh, crap! There goes my hope for a bogey!" Fascinatingly, my sand shots improved dramatically once I started this little mantra. I did not even believe the mantra. *I did not have to*—my brain bought into it anyway. But my positive, smiling attitude helped to improve my actual shots! Perhaps I was more relaxed, perhaps it was magic. It does not really matter why. Even if my shots were still awful, my experience of the sand became more enjoyable. I created the memory of "I am awesome out of the sand!" and the joke of it, so even if I did not make the shot, that happy moment infuses my memory.

> *Happiness is not a goal, it is a by-product.*
> *—Eleanor Roosevelt*

If you have joyous experiences, more joy will come from them, from the memory of them. Choose to create joy in your life, and it will come back to you again and again. It is truly the gift that keeps giving.

> *Tous les jours à tous points de vue je vais de mieux en mieux.*
> *Every day, in every way, I'm getting better and better.*
> *—Emil Coue, the father of autosuggestion*

This is a training technique for the brain. For years doctors have been telling their ill patients to repeat this mantra, or similar, when they get up each morning. Positive thinking produces positive results. By saying that phrase, they make it so.

To believe is very dull.
To doubt is intensely engrossing.
—Oscar Wilde

Many people practice life without intentional thought. They are sucked into their daily affairs, dealing with 'random' problems that are thrown their way, alternating between happiness and unhappiness. Because of cause and effect, we are all producers of the lives we live. Our thoughts create the energy that drives us. Bad thoughts eventually produce evil. Good thoughts create positive energy and nice experiences. You are the producer of your life's film. You are in charge. What do you want to see when you look back at your memories, at the film of your life? Will you tell your camera crew to go film at the dump, or to find the palace and the gardens? It is your conscious decision, which way you want to go for your images today and for your future. Most importantly, it is NEVER too late to change. There are plenty of ways to get to the gardens, even if you have spent your life until now examining the refuse in the river. You are the producer and you can order your camera crew wherever you want.

Finally, brothers, whatever is true, whatever is noble, what-
ever is right, whatever is pure, whatever is lovely, whatever is
admirable—if anything is excellent or praiseworthy—think
about such things. Whatever you have learned or received or
heard from me, or seen in me—put it into practice. And the
God of peace will be with you.
(Philippians 4:8-10)

I traveled through Africa and saw children living in abject poverty, who were happily playing in the dirt and mud. They had no basis of comparison to comprehend what they were lacking. They were oblivious to dissatisfaction because they did not know how badly off they were. In Hollywood the rich sit idly by their pools and complain about the filet mignon they had last night, because they have lost all perspective as well. It is all a state of mind. Most of us are doing extremely well, but we lose sight of that because of all the distractions of every day. Some of us find it easier to be dissatisfied than content. Donald Trump does not own 99.9 percent of New York real estate. Poor guy. If he only looks at what he does not have, he truly is a poor guy. But if he looks at his balance sheet, he is very rich. If we concentrate on what is missing in our lives, we are all in poverty. But if we choose to see what we have spiritually, materialistically, in our families and friends, we are all wealthy. Today, almost all "poor" households in the U.S. have at least one television, and more than half have air conditioning. They believe they are poor, because others have more TVs or bigger houses. Because they are better nourished, poor children in the U.S. grow up to be, on average, "one inch taller and ten pounds heavier than the American GIs who stormed the Normandy beaches in World War II."[11] Compared to the poor in India, America's poor are doing quite well, even if they choose to feel deficient.

Misery loves miserable company.

Some people have never developed the necessary filters in their brains to achieve happiness. They experience insults even when none were intended. Their default switch is set at 'disappointed' and that way they are seldom more disappointed than what they expect; but in reality, they are never over-pleased with what they have. I do not condemn people for exhibiting reasonable emotions, of course. It would be natural to regret and revisit the events leading up to a hospital admission, for instance. But life marches on, and your choice should center on finding happiness, rather than dwelling in misery. Granted, it is not an easy choice, with so many distractions, but it is a healthier choice long-term. The sooner the accident victim can get to hopefulness in his life, the better his life will be. Similarly, the longer he dwells in misery, the more comfortable he is there, and the less accessible he will be for joy to permeate.

Sadness invites all kind of dire associates to the party.

Once we develop a habit of negative thinking, we become less able to think neutrally. The negative thought is very powerful. It halts optimism and creativity, replacing it with despair. Once you are entrenched in this vicious cycle, you become comfortable in it, and then any positive news is unwelcome, as it disrupts your negative position. The negative thinker does not want someone to lift him up. He finds reassurance in his pain and his sadness. And he says, truthfully, that life is dark.

Applied happiness.

Just like with any habit, the good news is that you can retrain your brain away from the negativity. When you start to purpose-fully choose your thoughts and you make them good thoughts, your world, and your experience in it, improves. If you examine it on a purely rational level, it boils down to this:

Choose to like something, and you will like it more.

Teach yourself to look at good things and find the good in things as they are. Do not use your camera to photograph the garbage, but turn your lens toward the sparkling lights. This does not mean that there is no garbage in the Seine. It is there, but you are forced by no one to look at it. Or, if you just cannot help looking at it, clean it up! And be happy about the positive effect you are having because you are counterbalancing the negative forces with creative ones.

You shape your future with your thoughts.

When you are walking to your car alone at night, would you purposely go down an unlit and dangerous-looking alley? Of course not, because you recognize that you would be putting yourself at risk. Unnecessary risk. Looking at negative things and images is putting your psyche at risk; you need to shut those images out or shut them down when they come to you. You need to refuse them. Do not offer them a foothold. Once you start rejecting negative imagery you will find it easier to train your thoughts onto positive imagery. Since we become what we think, eventually you will turn yourself into a happier person. It is all within your control.

There are five main obstacles to happiness that need discussion (and eradication).

1) Worry
2) Regret
3) Criticism
4) Confusion / Distraction
5) Boredom

WORRY

The word *worry* comes from the Old English term *wyrgan*, which means "to choke" or "to strangle." How appropriate.

Break the worry habit.

What did worry ever create? What help was worry to anyone? Worrying is simply a waste of time, and in that sense it is evil. In order to break any habit, you must replace it with another one. I choose worshiping to assuage my worries. Worship and prayer leaves you less time, and less need, for worry. The Bible tells us to rely on

God in times of hardship. Once you break the habit of worry, it is easier to resist the temptation for it when it comes back. For some, worry is their comfort zone. It is their nicotine. It is challenging for them to accept an opposing belief system. For them, it is easier to rely on their old habits of thought. Worrying is a choice, much like happiness.

> *Do not be anxious about anything, but in everything,*
> *by prayer and petition, with thanksgiving,*
> *present your requests to God.*
> *(Philippians 4:7)*

REGRET

Regret wastes time.

Look forward, so you can see the doors opening, and free your mind to find new interests. Learn from mistakes, but do not focus on their negative imagery for longer than the lesson requires. Regret is simply a negative emotion, so it needs to be replaced by the positive counterpart. Rephrase, "I'm so stupid!" with, "I'll be smarter next time!"

CRITICISM

Many of us unwittingly opt to be negative. It is so much easier to criticize than to appreciate. There are two main reasons for this.

1. Superiority
2. Culpability

Criticizing makes the critic feel superior. The judge is always better than the subject—at least in his own mind. Being judgmental also removes the critic from culpability. By negatively commenting on a situation, he at once elevates himself and places blame elsewhere.

> *It is by logic that we prove, but by intuition that we discover.*
> *To know how to criticize is good, but to know how to create is better.*
> —*Henri Poincaré*

I have a friend in the entertainment industry who is constantly complaining about her agent. She writes letters to her agent, telling him what he should do, and why, to no avail. The agent simply does whatever he wants, all the while verbally placating my actress friend. It is unceasingly tedious, but I see that my friend somehow feels vindicated by the agent's lack of response, and continues her barrage of supplications. In other words, her attempts to get him to behave a certain way are her contribution, and her absolution, allowing her to put all the blame on his failure to perform.

> *Insanity: doing the same thing over and over again*
> *and expecting different results.*
> —*Rita Mae Brown.*

My friend comes to me and says, "My agent never follows through when I ask him to do something." Initially, I told her to change agents. "They're all the same," she would answer. "You don't really know that. Sometimes you have to kiss a lot of frogs." But she refused to change agents. So then I told her to stop asking, if the answer was always "no." "Oh, no. He always says 'yes,' but never follows through." I suggested that a 'yes' that means the same as 'no' is, in fact, a 'no.' That seemed too far a leap for her. I suppose it is obvious by now that I was screaming, "Abort! Abort! Abort!"

inside, but here is what I did: I told her I would not discuss her agent problems anymore. That, at least, removed me from the equation, and I am much happier for it.

> *Some cause happiness wherever they go;*
> *others whenever they go.*
> *—Oscar Wilde*

You cannot pre-chew food for people. They must eat for themselves. But you can serve them bread and milk. You can show them the Truth and then it is upon them to accept it or reject it. You can lead someone toward happiness, but they have to personally seek it and choose it. It is a process and it is work. My actress friend has not yet realized that the blame still rests entirely with her and her actions. In time it is possible she will understand her own role in her unhappiness. Free from the burden of discussing her displeasure about her agent, our conversations have become much more interesting and cheerful. Eventually, I hope that she may comprehend how removing the negativity resulted in happier times for us, and could do the same for her.

Break the criticism habit.

Instead of ceaselessly criticizing, look for the positive, and remove the negative. Work for change by trying something, but once you identify a failure, do not endlessly criticize that disappointment. Simply change the request to invite a success. Everyone will be happier for it.

Always a critic, never to create.

CONFUSION / DISTRACTION

I had a friend who fell in love with a guy who lived in a foreign country. She was in her thirties, a working woman with a great career, but one that would not translate well to that small town abroad. He asked her to marry him, and she really wanted to, but she was trying to figure out how to preserve her career while traveling back and forth from the U.S. There was a great deal of confusion, juggling all the various elements to find an equation that worked. Eventually, she simplified it into one decision: what was most important in her life? She chose love and married him, and forewent the extra stress of travel and separation in order to pursue their relationship.

Sometimes you just cannot have it all, and those who say you can are lying. You can have a piece of pie, but to eat the entire pie after a complete dinner is ridiculous. To try to chase after one dream at the expense of another often ensures losing both. We are only human, after all. Once the decision was made, life got much simpler and less stressful for my friend, and she was able to make the most of living in a foreign country, and pursuing other goals as well. Sacrificing one thing to obtain something more valuable does not mean sacrificing everything else. There are always other options, if you open your heart to finding them. My friend left her career but discovered another love, and, eventually, another career that was completely different from her first one. Now she has a successful career and a happy marriage because she was willing to dedicate herself to one dream, entirely, in order to protect it.

BOREDOM

Deficiency forces development.

If you have your house, family, everything you ever wanted, what is your impetus to get up in the morning or to do anything? Even if you have everything you want right now, the world changes. Your friends change, your family's needs change. Your children provide you with immense motivation because of your commitment to provide for them. With total satisfaction comes boredom. A lot of us would be happy for a little boredom for a while, but not for too long!

After high school in Austria, I traveled to North Africa to establish a concrete and aggregate business. Its success eventually took me to Saudi Arabia, where I spent years building the business and making my fortune. But for that time, that is all I did. Because of the laws of the land, in Saudi Arabia, I was denied even simply a normal life, much less any luxury. There was no social life, no friends, no women, and I basically lived my work. My time over there was miserable, and I was exhausted from all my efforts. So when I left it behind, I felt like I had some catching up to do. I bought myself a yacht. I had a captain, a steward and a mate, and I lived the life that most people only dream about.

> *Es ist nichts so schwehr zu ertragen wie ein paar sorgenfreie tagen.*
> *Nothing is so hard to bear as many days without a care.*
> *—Johann Wolfgang von Goethe*

It was Tuesday morning and they had set breakfast up on the upper deck, with croissants, melon and prosciutto and fine coffee. I looked at my fabulous motorcycle and I sighed and said to myself this is really great. The sun is shining, summer is here, I have my bike and no demands on me. Four weeks later, I was still on my boat in a different port, with other friends and I still said, "Wow, this is really great." It was Tuesday or maybe Wednesday, or, I suppose, Thursday; but it was a great day. Wonderful. After three months of that fabulous time, without any purposefulness, the emptiness started to set in on me. I finally had to admit that my life was vacant. I had needed the down time to relax after what had been an extremely stressful time in Saudi Arabia, but once I had re-acclimated, I simply could not sit idle anymore. Humans are programmed to go out and do, to achieve, to decide. Those who do not, eventually find they are lost.

What we envision as necessary for our happiness, and what actually inspires happiness are often two very different things.

People put on a façade and go out, and they look happy. Have you ever gone to a party or a bar with people who are drunk? Initially, they all look like they are having a good time, but eventually you start seeing the truth, which is desperation. They are desperate for something to make them happy, because they have not found the way to do it themselves. And in their despair, they discover that escapism (drinking) provides them with a respite from their unhappiness. The party face does not permeate to the inside, where they are despondent. When they get home and get into bed, the makeup is off and the party is over, and the truth comes out.

Just as people invite sadness or frustrations into their lives, they can also invite happiness. But the idea that a new car or a night at the dance club is enough for your sustained happiness is ridiculous, though that does not stop people from believing it. Superficial happiness is almost worse than none at all. It is like a tease.

If only I were in better shape. If only I could be younger. If only I were better looking. How can a person ever achieve happiness if they only concentrate on the external, superficial issues? Do not be deceived by "if only." Health is not the secret to happiness. There are a lot of healthy people who are miserable. Money is not the secret, either. Many rich people are lonely and dissatisfied. Beauty is not the key. Of course, these trappings may be nice. Nobody would argue that having money, good looks and good health are all blessings, but those traits are not as important as our society wants us to believe. Happiness can only come from within, a choice bolstered by hope and love. All those insubstantial qualities that we crave are distractions for our minds and temptations for our hearts. Eventually we must look inside to discover whether what we have in our hearts is sufficiently fertile for joy to take root. Once we have planted our joy in rich, spiritual earth, none of those external things are necessary. I am not knocking them or promoting them. I am saying that they are inconsequential to true happiness, and sometimes they are the obstacles to finding it.

A life directed mainly towards the fulfillment of personal desires
sooner or later always leads to bitter disappointment.
—Albert Einstein[12]

While happiness is very much a choice, the second, equally important ingredient for happiness is hope, our next chapter.

There is only one cause of unhappiness:
the false beliefs you have in your head,
beliefs so widespread, so commonly held,
that it never occurs to you to question them.
—Anthony de Mello[13]

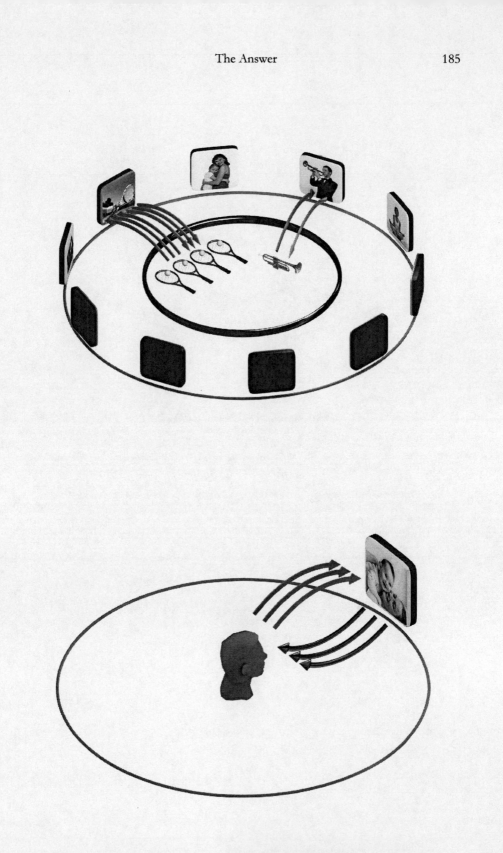

We become what we think. We become what we invite into ourselves, from the infinite possibilities this life offers us. Some of us, for example, want to play tennis, and decide to play and practice and therefore improve. Some of us invite evil and evil takes hold of us to the degree we invite it. Some of us choose to turn to good and to God, and we are enlightened to the degree we desire Him.

Chapter 17

Is There Hope For Me?

*If you want to build a ship, don't herd people together to
collect wood and don't assign them tasks and work, but rather
teach them to long for the endless immensity of the sea.*
—Antoine de Saint-Exupery

Hope is the most essential ingredient for any creative endeavor.
Hope is the inspirational power that urges us to be productive and
good. The mother gets up and hopes that today is a good day for
her children. Through hope, she helps them to plan their futures.
The architect starts his day hoping to build a great building. Hope
is the force that compels us to get back up again after we have
fallen. Even though we may fail or make a million mistakes, hope
tempts us to give it one more try. Hope lets us believe in ourselves
and sleep well, content in the knowledge that tomorrow we can try
again.

Once you choose hope, anything's possible.
—Christopher Reeve

The only reason any happiness can exist is hope. Optimism
gives us the impetus to try, to invent, to solve, and to create.

Optimism can be learned, since we all live in a world that is a virtual creation of our minds. My house, no matter how strong I build it, will eventually crumble. My family, once I pass on, will be taken from me, as will my clothes, jewelry, money, and all my possessions. I know that as a certainty, as I know I will die. But through the teachings of Jesus Christ I have faith and I have hope, and that is what keeps me creating and recreating myself spiritually. There is no happiness in great loss, but for the Christian, death is not loss, after all. The spiritual achievements gained during your lifetime are not lost to anything, and you cannot lose your love either, as love is also transcendent. With the grace of God, nothing will be lost in death, and in that knowledge resides hope. It is the bulwark upon which true happiness may thrive.

God's love gives us hope.

Since your demise is inevitable, there can be no true happiness without an understanding of where you go when you die. Christ answers this question precisely. He is the only one to give an answer at all. For that reason, His is the only path to happiness. Other answers are incomplete or unsatisfying, or nothing. If there is nothing, then we are all waiting for death to turn us into dust, and there can be only fleeting glimpses of happiness, but none of it profound or true.

Hope is the confidence that things will turn out the way they should.

When you get into an elevator and you press the number three button, do you know you will get to the third floor? Not exactly. Your experience dictates that you will arrive on three, but the elevator may break, or may fail, or it could turn into a time machine and take you back to 1967. Ending up on the third floor seems to be the most reasonable assumption, but pushing that button is an act of faith. There are many things you put your faith in. You believe you will go on vacation, or that you will eat a very good breakfast on Saturday, or that the milk is unspoiled. You believe you will live to see your next birthday. Most of your beliefs come true because you are conditioned only to expect reasonable things. These beliefs are founded on both reason and hope.

Without hope, reason has little value.

Suppose today you have everything your heart has ever desired, with all your dreams fulfilled. Now, say you learn with certainty that tomorrow you will die. Your joy vanishes. Once the hope for tomorrow is gone, so is happiness. If you knew that tomorrow you would lose everything, what good would your possessions serve today? Sure, you might enjoy a few bites of your favorite pie, but it would only serve as contrast to the fact that it would be your last piece of pie, and you would have little appetite. Time also begins to lose meaning. After the doctor assures you of only days or months to live, what is there left for you?

Death is always there, waiting for you. It may be right around the corner, or it may be decades away, but rest assured that it awaits you in the end. As humans we can delude ourselves into ignoring the plain fact of death, for years if necessary. That is why young people can be so rash and imprudent. They have not yet understood that death comes to anyone at any time. They do not consider themselves "anyone" and they feel like they can live forever. This sentiment is good enough for most of us through our 20s and 30s, and even well into our 40s. But as we approach old age, hope for tomorrow diminishes, because the weight, the finality of our impending fate descends upon us. With looming mortality, hope for tomorrow becomes restricted. The expectations and joyfulness of ongoing life is inhibited by the fear of death. In younger years the significant question of purpose can be easily placed on the back burner for a while. As we age, though, we are gradually and more insistently confronted by our mortality. It stares us down, daring us to blink. That is when we start to delve more into the purpose of life, searching for the essential answers that religion (instead of mainstream science) can provide.

> *Jesus said, "I am the resurrection and the life.*
> *He who believes in me, though he may die, he shall live.*
> *And whoever lives and believes in me shall never die ..."*

That is the most hopeful of messages, because it debunks death. Death is often equated with despair, hopelessness, and desolation. The morbid fear of death is completely counteracted in the Christian faith by Christ telling us to follow Him and receive everlasting life. He said that whoever believed in Him could not die, and then He showed us his power through His own resurrection. He *overcame* death, rose again, and promised life eternal to His followers. From His teachings, together with the lessons we have in the laws of the universe, we learn that we need not fear death. Far from being the opposite of life, death is actually a part of life, a different phase of life. His message intends to destroy the enemy of hope, *fear*, and demolish anxiety and worry.

If you believe, death will not touch you.

Christ is the only religious leader to have said this and done the things for which He is credited. There are other religious leaders, good people who share great messages, but no human individual has ever done even a small percentage of the things ascribed to Jesus Christ.

Without a belief in Christ and His teachings of hope, happiness is truly ephemeral. You can be happy sometimes, even a lot, but ultimately, who will hold your hand at your deathbed, but Christ? In Christ we find hope for our souls and understand that they endure even though our physical bodies do not. We know where we are going and we are promised a heaven that is greater than our imaginations can encompass. That is all good, hopeful news.

In essence, if you believe, not only will you lose nothing, but you will gain everything, and eternal life.

Chapter 18

How Should I Face My Doubts?

A little philosophy inclineth man's mind to atheism,
but depth in philosophy bringeth men's minds about to religion.
—Francis Bacon

Doubt is a great catalyst for gaining knowledge. Your doubt compels you to investigate. Your doubt perhaps inspired you to buy this book. Doubt is an instigator, not a destroyer, as many believe. Embrace doubt, because it provides the energy of thought, which invites discovery.

Doubt is the mortar among the bricks of knowledge.

I had long talks with a Catholic priest who revealed to me his fear of death. He was devout, but also doubtful. Doubt is not a contradiction to faith, but an opportunity for affirmation. After we talked about the laws of the universe and the cycle of life, where death follows life, and so life follows death, he discovered that his faith in one precipitated his faith in the other. He had simply forgotten the second half. There is always a key to unlock the doubt and set it free. That confirmation of his ultimate overriding faith, gave his belief an added dimension. The doubt, which compelled him to delve further, returned a dividend of strengthened faith.

I respect faith, but doubt is what gets you an education.
—Wilson Mizner

I built a wall against enemy invaders, but I was not sure of its strength, so I added another layer of stone. Still, I was unconvinced of its fortitude, so I added yet another layer. My doubt triggered me to make the wall strong enough to withstand the coming assault. The priest bolstered his faith with another layer of reassurance, because of his small doubts about death.

Doubt is the opportunity for growth in faith. It throws down a gauntlet that should be picked up and answered. Christopher Columbus doubted the prevailing theory that the world was flat, and insisted on testing his own belief in the roundness of the earth. Lo and behold, he discovered land across the ocean and a new faith in himself.

God shows his mercy every day on those who curse and deny him.

Generally, there are two names in which to categorize people who do not believe in any God. Agnostic, a term originated by the scientist T.H. Huxley in the 1800s, identifies someone for whom that fundamental question of God has no answer. Although there are many different versions of agnosticism, most agnostics prefer to abstain from the debate about God because it is too uncomfortable or too oppressive. They choose to ignore the question, probably because, if they do not fall to either side, they feel safer. The complacency of "willful blindness" is the term C. S. Lewis coined. I have my own name for it: "cop-out." To ignore the question of God is to ignore life itself. This question, this debate, is like the elephant in the room. It is roaring, but some choose not to hear it. It smells, yet some say there is no odor. Agnostics admit there might be an animal in the room, but they do not know what kind, and they cover their eyes and ears and close their noses.

The other kind of non-believer is the atheist. An *a-theist* is someone who lacks a belief in God, or who strongly believes there can be no such thing. This form of thought (it can hardly be called a belief) came about in the 1700s and was fueled by Darwin's Theory of Evolution, although he himself was never known to be an atheist. Darwin struggled fiercely to reconcile his radical new concept of evolution with the religious beliefs to which he subscribed. He knew that evolution would test religious faith, and was reluctant to announce his findings, until another scientist, Alfred Wallace, began circulating similar views. Once he realized that these discoveries would unavoidably be revealed he decided to publish his findings. While it added much to the debate about the existence of a divine being, Darwin's Theory of Evolution by no means supplants God.

The atheist is frozen in an infantile tantrum of denial.

There is a principle in theatrical improvisation that says, "never deny—always be moving the plot along." In other words, if in the scene your partner says you are the village idiot, then by golly, you become the village idiot and ask where they put the sky. The tacit agreement is to accept and expand the discussion, because a denial stops the scene. "God does not exist" halts any dialog. Just as agnosticism fairly begs for conversation, atheism is so entrenched in disbelief that it pleads for isolation. And isolation is what atheists discover, because their conviction removes hope. They replace God with what? Nothing. Eternal darkness. And it is nothing that they have to look forward to upon their deaths. Atheism is by definition a negative. Though usually too cumbersome for younger people, the important questions become more poignant as one ages and nears the end of one's life. The atheist is hit by the futility of it all. What is the point, after all, if there is nothing else but this world and all its selfishness and hostility? I imagine the majority of suicides are atheists.

Let's Make a Deal!

There are two doors. Behind Door Number One is life everlasting in paradise with all your loved ones and the greatest joy imaginable, in permanent communion with God. And Behind Door Number Two lurks death, destruction, and separation from all your loved ones eternally. Supreme hope versus ultimate hopelessness. You are faced with choosing between these two doors. Picture them. Door One is labeled "Hope" and Door Two is marked "Despair." Which door will you choose?

Every day you are faced with the choice to believe, to investigate, or to ignore.

Christianity teaches hope and love; atheism teaches absolute darkness.

Atheists, as they age, become despondent, hopeless individuals. They have no choice, unfortunately. Their loneliness gets more pronounced as they age, since in the end they see themselves as completely lost. They may argue that death is the ultimate "release," and since there is nothing after that, it is comforting in that finality; but when one looks at the black chasm that atheists perceive as death, it is anything but comforting. As their friends die off, all they experience is the pain of the loss and the abandonment. For them there is no hope in death. We cannot blame them for getting dispirited (pardon the pun).

Then again, why? Why close yourself off to a possibility, however remote, that God is there? If you are stranded on a deserted island, far from any civilization, would you simply give up any hope of discovery and rescue? Even the worst pessimist must admit it would be a happier choice to believe that help might possibly arrive. Well, that is God in a nutshell, as if you could put Him in one!

The committed atheist functions within three extremes: fear, anger and ego. Either his ego simply will not allow for the existence of God, he is too angry to desire a belief, or he is too afraid to accept a God more powerful than himself. Self-reliant to a fault, it is inevitable that at some point he becomes helpless, whether it is due to worldly circumstances or purely the ravages of age and poor health. One thing that a good atheist has is the ability to commit. He stays his path until the pain becomes so great that either that pain destroys him or he screams out for help. It is similar to drug addiction, but the addiction is to self: ego. An eleventh-hour acceptance of God as divine power would represent a fundamental change. The last thing an atheist wants to hear is that for 50 or more years of his life he closed himself off to a force that actually does exist, to a truth that saves, and to a death that means life.

Atheism = Isolation

What of the effort that atheists put into their arguments? That effort would be better spent in fair-minded research. It is, after all, extremely difficult to prove a negative. "There is, beyond any doubt, no God." How do you get *there*? They make an assumption of supreme intelligence that is incredibly egotistical. They are saying, in essence, that they have been everywhere in the universe, and have not seen life anywhere. Therefore, they continue erroneously, there is no intelligent life out in the universe. The first assumption was already wrong. They moan that it is impossible to prove God. In this book, I logically prove His existence. You may doubt some of my corollaries, but I assure you there is absolutely no substantial proof of "no God." To conclude with absoluteness that there is no God is negative and naïve, counterproductive and, finally, illogical. The atheist attempts to demonstrate his superiority, but instead proves only his foolishness.

A lack of proof is no proof, yet.

When our candle is long and strong, and we have all of life ahead of us, tomorrow always looks like a great thing. We fail to consider eternity or need God. Our uncertainties are insignificant in our daily lives. But when our candle burns shorter, and hardship assaults us, we may be divorcing, sick or aging, then we contemplate the *end*. For those with skepticism, there is hope. There is an invitation to find answers and affirmation. Ignoring doubt only serves to intensify it and its accompanying fears. An intelligent person faces his doubts by embracing them, exploring them, investigating their source and mollifying them.

So, what about those very intelligent scientists, who use their science, the study of the physical, to disprove a being that is purely spiritual?

> *"God is spirit and his worshipers must*
> *worship in the spirit and in the truth."*
> (John 4:24)

If a man studies French for many years, but has never studied Chinese, he knows nothing about the Chinese language, its structure, symbols or poets. Being completely ignorant of the Chinese language, this language cannot make sense to him. Now, imagine this Francophile loudly proclaiming that the Chinese language, to which he has never bothered exposing himself and which he does not understand, therefore does not exist.

Brilliant.

The prestigious US National Academy of Science has gone on record with the following statement:

> *"Science is a way of knowing about the natural world. It is*
> *limited to explaining the natural world through natural causes.*
> *Science can say nothing about the supernatural world through*
> *natural causes. Whether God exists or not is a question about*
> *which science is neutral."*[4]

But that doesn't prevent any number of scientists from weighing in with their *opinions*, using their vaulted positions to advance a theory on which they've done precious little research, from Michael Faraday to James Clark Maxwell and Arno Penzias, many scientists obviously feel qualified to speak on a subject they don't study.

There are also numerous, leading scientists from the past and present, who have openly professed their faith in God. They see the perfect complement science provides to faith.

> *In view of such harmony in the Cosmos, which I, with my*
> *limited human mind, am able to recognize, there are yet*
> *people who say there is no God. But what really makes me*
> *angry is that they quote me for the support of such views.*
> *—Albert Einstein*[15]

Michael Behe, an American biochemist and professor, gives a simply brilliant argument supporting intelligent design in his "irreducible complexity argument."

Behe suggests that complex, biological systems cannot be engineered simply through natural selection. He offers as proof a traditional mousetrap. For such a device to function, it has a specific number of components: a base, hammer, spring, trapping arm, and the catch that holds it open, without which it would cease to work. That is called irreducible—because if any one of these components is missing or even unmatched to the others, the mousetrap won't be a mousetrap any more. Behe notes that many biological systems are similarly comprised of several indispensible parts, without which they cannot perform or benefit their owner.

Can natural selection build this type of system up, bit by bit? No says Behe, because natural selection, by the nature of the theory, wouldn't operate on a biological system that performs no survival related function. In this case there is nothing to *select*. A mousetrap that contains its base, hammer and release mechanism, but is without a spring, is non-functional and of no value to its owner. Natural selection would dispose of it long before accidentally fitting it with a spring to make it functional.

There is another facet of this argument that is seldom considered.

If there was no thought, this book would not exist.
If there was no good, there would be no evil.
If there was no light, there could be no darkness.
If there was no birth, there would be no death.
If there was no mother, her daughter would not exist.
Without the + there is no −.
Without right there is no wrong.
If there is no creator, there can be no creation.
Without God, there is no atheism.

The everlasting laws of cause and effect and the all-encompassing law of polarity show us that atheists were also created by God, even if they dispute that fact.

Although atheistic scientists argue against the existence of God, they would never argue that $0+0=1$. Yet that, in effect, is their argument against God. In order to arrive at 1, there must have been a 1 somewhere in the beginning. You cannot create a 1 out of a zero.

The atheist's principle problem is his infantile arrogance. How can he watch a film on his TV if he refuses to press the power button and turn it on? Atheists face a blank screen and then victoriously proclaim that there is no program running, while refusing to look for the remote. They never push the power button to invite the film, the information, to be shown to them.

Imagine walking on a steep mountain hike through the Austrian Alps. As we climb higher and higher above the tree line, we are picking our way through a breathtaking maze of irregular rock formations. Boulders, enormous and small, line our path and rise in front of us.

Suddenly, we come around a bend and see the most amazing sight, right there in front of us, in the middle of the mountain. In the midst of the boulders and rocks there is what appears to be a staircase chiseled into the mountainside: twenty-five steps, cut perfectly into this rough, windswept, rocky slope. You happen to have a small measuring tape in your Swiss army knife, so we measure the width of the stairs and each riser. To our surprise each stair is an exact copy of the others, all perfectly aligned with similar dimensions, but they are sitting in the middle of nowhere.

What are we to conclude? There is no human life to be seen, no old campfires to testify to the builder, none of his trash, or his drawings or tools left beside the stairs. And yet, our first (and only) question would be, "Who carved these stairs and why?" We would immediately agree that these steps bear absolute witness to someone's work, even though we cannot see anyone or even evidence of anyone there, because, although we have no explanation, even the crudest logic would presume that *someone* created them, though the *reason* may evade us.

But the atheist, by facile extension of his or her standard argument, would simply stare in wonder at the amazing nature that crafted the incredible staircase merely by chance!

Now consider that these steps, hewn out of the sheer rock face of the mountain, are comparatively simplistic, next to a single human blood cell, or the complexity of a human kidney, or to the unbelievably complex construct of a human eye.

It's amusing that when examining the example of steps carved into a rock formation the atheist quickly concludes that only an intelligent being could have performed such a feat of engineering, and yet when we talk about an equation that is infinitely more complex, suddenly chance and the randomness of nature are incredible creators that complete a task infinitely more complex than a simple exercise in carving.

An even simpler example would be the following: You left your house in a hurry to go out of town for a few days after you threw a birthday party for a good friend. The house was a total mess. All the rooms were used, the beds slept in, the bathroom towels left lying on the floor, the kitchen strewn with broken glasses and dirty plates. You get the picture; the house was a complete mess.

When you return five days later, the house is miraculously clean and neat. Complete order. The beds are all made; the bathrooms are pristine, as is the kitchen. The fridge has been cleaned out; dishes washed and arranged in the cupboards, the broken glasses replaced. Even the back yard is now perfectly cleaned. So the house went from disorder to order. And even though you don't know who created this "order" it must have been some pretty great cleaning service, certainly.

How certain? Well, 100 percent certain. What spontaneously returns from disorder to order, without any outside influence? Nothing in nature, of course, except, for the atheist, apparently, everything. Their argument would state the more complex a task gets, such as the creation of life, the more reliable the nothingness that creates it.

Some scientists are extraordinarily limited in their findings of eternal knowledge, but certain in their belief that God does not exist.

Imagine a timeline, starting with, for the scientist's sake, the Big Bang, and ending 10,000 years in the future. It is a mile long. Humanity's study of science occupies a small part of that timeline, perhaps six inches or a foot. A mere 500 years ago, science, by today's standard, knew very, very little, and much of that "knowledge" was wrong. (Remember all the sciences, like alchemy, that are no longer even considered science?)

Yet, from their point of view, science had reached monumental achievements:

Nicolas Copernicus's (1473-1543) work, *De Revolutionibus Orbium Coelestium* (1543), laid the foundation for all modern astronomy, while challenging the prevailing assumption that Earth was the center of the universe and drawing strict criticism from the scientific community. Now we look at his detractors with disdain, but back then they were the standard-bearers of science, and nobody to trifle with.

Robert Boyle (1627-1691) rejected the long-standing practices and hopes of what was then modern science: medieval alchemy. He established the foundations of modern chemistry and provided the first definition of a chemical element, a chemical reaction, and chemical analysis. This went completely against the accepted science of the time. He was a ground-breaker, but now his theories are considered elementary.

Isaac Newton (1642-1727), regarded by many as the father of modern physics, explained the working of gravity and was instrumental in developing the calculus. His work, *Principia*, was the most advanced and sweeping scientific treatise of his day. Today it is considered only the *basis* for modern physics.

Gregor Mendel (1822-1884) is viewed as the father of modern genetics because of his work explaining the hybridization of plants. Did he ever dream of mapping the human genome? It probably never occurred to him, and yet that's exactly what our modern science has accomplished.

Today's scientists are rightfully as proud of their achievements as their colleagues were 500 years ago, but we view those antiquated scientists and some of their discoveries as outdated and old-fashioned, because their knowledge was still at the beginning of the evolution of their fields. Look at, for instance, quantum physics, the microchip, or a smart phone. None of those former, laudable geniuses would be able to weigh in on what we lay people now take for granted.

Using our timeline, imagine what scientists in the future might think about the state of science today, not in five or ten feet but in a hundred feet or a thousand feet from us. Assuming we have not self-destructed, those future scientists would smile a pitiful smile at the very low level of intelligence that science has currently achieved.

But 10,000 years from today, the "Sermon on the Mount" by Jesus Christ will have as much validity today as it had 2,000 years ago.

That is the difference between science and religion.

Science, as necessary as it is, is constantly searching to explain the unknown, and when it has discovered a small slice of new materialistic knowledge that God has laid out, like bait, for it to finally uncover, it proudly proclaims to be so much closer to Knowledge (with a capital K).

And this is where science errs so profoundly. Many hundreds of years ago, scientists thought they were very close to finding the knowledge that would give them the secret to changing any metal into gold, alchemy. They also believed they could gain the knowledge of everything. They figured they just needed to open one more door and … Eureka! To their astonishment, behind that one door were another ten doors. So, they took up the task to open those ten doors only to find a hundred more doors behind every door they opened. And behind those doors were again perhaps 10,000 more. In a way, the closer they came in their quest for knowledge, the farther they found themselves from gaining the knowledge they sought. The creator of this universe is so much greater than his creation and so much greater than even imaginable. Science and human scientists are at a complete disadvantage.

Think how the scientists and lay-people of the distant future will judge the science we have today, and imagine that none of them will ever, through science, scratch the surface of the creative force we know as God.

You sit in a dark room.
Open the curtains, and the darkness must yield to the light.
You may doubt that the sun is shining,
but if you do not investigate and open the curtains,
you will still just be sitting in darkness.

Chapter 19

Why Can't I Just Be Spiritual?

Saying you are smart does not make you smart,
And calling yourself spiritual does not make you spiritual.

Do you believe in the 'forces of the universe?' This is like believing in the forces of grass or a tree. If you believe that plants grow because of some spiritual force, that information is meaningless unless it brings you somewhere. People who sort of believe in something but cannot really define it have simply not thought a lot about it. Perhaps they are scared, or lazy, or just apathetic, but as this book shows, the answers are there if you are willing to open your eyes and look.

God as Christ came into this world and told us exactly how our lives should be. He explained our purpose and proposed the best methods to achieve it, through the Lord's Prayer. He said to follow in His footsteps and He freely took human sin upon Himself and died in order for mankind to achieve his glory with God. No tree or stone has ever done that. Nature does not give a crap about you, but God does. Natural forces are not creative by themselves. In fact, according to the law of entropy, nature is destructive. Life force, or the love of God, is the only constructive force in the universe.

I took a day to search for God,
And found Him not; but as I trod,
By rocky ledge, through woods untamed,
Just where one scarlet lily flamed,
I saw His footprint in the sod
—William Bliss Carmen

Imagine walking on the beach with your father. He tells you that he loves you but that he must leave soon. Still, he wants to maintain a strong relationship with you. When he leaves, he gives you his direct line and asks you to call him as often as feasible so you two can remain close. But once he is gone, instead of finding a phone, you go back to the beach and find the imprint his foot left in the sand. Instead of calling him, sharing your adventures and problems, and otherwise seeking his presence in your life, you sit and wonder at the beauty of the grains and how they were molded in the shape of his bare foot. It is foolishness to imagine that a relationship with mindless sand, which simply reacted to the footstep, could substitute for connection with a living, loving God. The Universe, nature, can only react to God's creation but it is not creative by itself. The Universe is the mindless stage of a play, but not the author.

Appearances are everything, they say.
To eternity, appearances are nothing.

Two men relax together in a cottage in the French Alps, bragging. "I am a great ski racer," says the first one. "I am also a fantastic ski racer," counters the second man. They sing their own praises to each other over hot chocolate all day and half the night. What good is all that boasting if they never get out to race? If you do not ski race, then you are not a ski racer, no matter how much you may claim to be one.

I believe, but I'm too busy/lazy/disinterested to investigate any further than that.

If you are merely "spiritual" and your version of spirituality does not actually demand any particular behavior, then what good is it? What purpose does it serve, save to make you feel interesting and of value? It feels good to declare spiritual leanings. Particularly these days, it gives us an aura of sophistication, much like the do-gooder who proclaims his belief in global warming. But if the climate change enthusiast does not actually ride his bike everywhere, then, really, where is his concern, except on his hypocritical sleeve for all to see? He is like the guy who attends AA meetings for the business connections. Claiming you are spiritual is akin to professing love for someone in a faraway country, who you never see or correspond with. It may feel good to say you are in love, but it is meaningless if you will not move mountains to be with the object of your desire.

Those who can't, teach.

Some people talk more than perform. If you can do something, why sit around gabbing about it all the time? Go and do it! If Tiger Woods stopped playing golf, we would not call him a golfer anymore, we would say he *was* a golfer. Similarly, you are not spiritual, or religious, if you do not actively practice. Spirituality without action is one of the flattest and most empty things in the world.

> *The Christian idea has not been tried and found wanting.*
> *It has been found difficult-and left untried.*
> *—G.K. Chesterton*

In the days and weeks following 9/11, the churches, synagogues, and other houses of worship were full. A traumatized people craved the connection with a supreme being as they searched for comfort and security in a suddenly unpredictable and perilous world. Those senseless terrorist events served to motivate even marginal believers to connect with God in the most tangible way possible. To this end, they did not, most of them, run into the woods to convene with the trees and wind, to join with the "Universe." They could no longer afford to be "interesting" or pretend to have deep thoughts. They had the strong desire for a connection to God, and for that they attended churches. Church affords an authentic link to God that is much more difficult to attain elsewhere, because the church can provide a definition and a veracity from its history, which cannot be found elsewhere. Spirituality is the sallow cousin of true religious dedication. You can try it, but it will never measure up.

The way to feel connected to God is through prayer and deed. If you profess to have faith in God, then I hope you are sufficiently awed, overawed, by His magnificence and munificence. Once you determine His validity and His power, it seems inconceivable to stop there. He is accessible and desirous of a relationship with you, so how can you turn down that invitation? If Tiger Woods (or any other mega-star) phoned you, would you refuse the call? If you were invited backstage to meet Britney or Mick or the President, would you decline? Of course not. People are drawn to power, even as they are frightened by it.

Acknowledge God—then choose between self and service.

Somehow we get caught up in the "reality" of this world, and forget that there is an even greater universe out there—the universe created by God's love. God is bigger than all the stars put together, and He invites you to regularly converse with Him. Do not rely on being "spiritual," because it is not enough. On the contrary, it is an insult to ignore Him when you know He is there at the door, waiting. If no one told you Tiger was on the phone, he could not blame you for not picking it up. You were programmed from your birth into the human race to deliberately and systematically search out your creator, as every society on record has done. So, once you know, you may no longer trip along aimlessly and ignore the facts.

It is specious to argue that God is unfamiliar and therefore my faith is weak. It is self-defeating. In order to believe, it is necessary to become familiar. You do not get to know your neighbors by avoiding them. You invite conversation with them on the street, at the mailbox, or when you walk you dog. Then you have them over for coffee or for dinner. You cultivate that familiarity, sometimes simply because it feels better to know who is living next door, for your own comfort. Of course, it will take some time for the friendship to build enough for you to spend the holidays together, for instance.

Why should it be any different for a relationship with God? He needs an invitation. He gave you free choice. Do you believe he would then just hang over your shoulder jabbering at you, trying to get a response? No, of course not. In fact, if your neighbor did that to you, always hanging out at your front door when you came home, or peeking in the window for a chat during dinner, you would get quite annoyed. God needs to be sought out and asked over for coffee.

A parent raises his child to be an honest, upstanding citizen and to love life, not to do drugs or drink. Then, he sends the child off to college, waiting, with bated breath, the phone call asking for help or advice, though preferring the call to be simply for a talk and catch up. The parent stays home, ready, at the other end of the phone line. He pines for a steady connection with the child throughout that child's adult life.

> *We praise God not for his benefits, but for our own.*
> *–Thomas Aquinas*

God gave us the Ten Commandments, the Old Testament, and then, as humanity was still struggling to get it right, He came to us in the form of Jesus. He arrived to reinterpret the rules for us, partly so we would no longer be confused as to how to lead a righteous life, partly to model for us the Father-Son relationship. Now God waits for the phone calls, hoping they may be just to chat, but He is certainly available to offer counseling and help. Simply because God is everywhere, does not mean He imposes His presence. It would be impolite, like the parent showing up on campus and following his kid around to make sure he finds the library and does his homework. God chooses NOT to interfere, but to wait until He is summoned. Then and only then, He is already there, of course.

REPETITION

Rome was not built in a day.

In this simple, common phrase lives the law of repetition. Whatever exists is because of one repetitive motion, or several. It is the recurring motion that builds. A car, a house, the earth, the solar system were not built instantaneously, but through repeated motion.

The famous painter, Vermeer, probably completed only two or three paintings a year. He would start with a vision of what he intended to paint. Then he would work out on paper how this idea would be translated to the canvas. His technique, *pointillism*, required layering the paint onto his canvas in small brush strokes, over and over. It gave the painting a three-dimensional effect. He would paint countless small brush strokes over months until finally he was satisfied, and the painting became known as a masterpiece.

Anything we do in life is filled with repetition. We get up, brush our teeth, eat breakfast, go to work, dial phone numbers. We all have some sort of bedtime ritual. Repetition is our foundation, our comfort, and our refuge.

You are looking for a doctor to perform surgery, so you ask, "How many times have you done this procedure?"

"None, and I really don't have any experience in performing any surgery of this kind, even."

"Uh, no, thank you. I'll find someone who knows what they're doing!" How many of us would entrust our care to a novice? Conversely, if the doctor's response were "several thousand," your comfort level would go right up because you would know you were in capable hands. A person cannot wish to become a surgeon, go to one class, and then take the exam. Internships and residencies are part of medical training, so student doctors can get better acquainted with procedures and practices, through repetition.

Repetition builds knowledge, confidence, and familiarity. Now, there is a magnificent word.

Familiarity:
  1. *a thorough knowledge and understanding of something, or*
  2. *closeness and friendliness in a personal relationship*
  3. *the quality of being familiar*[6]

I ask the person who does not believe in God if they have invited God into their lives. After puzzled reflection the person will often admit he has not. He may say he has never felt any real connection to God. This is the person who only goes to church on Easter and Christmas, which, frankly, is like playing on a tennis court twice and still expecting to play like Agassi or Graf.

If you want to know current events you turn on the TV and watch the news. You listen to reporters' accounts of the daily happenings, and you learn. Slowly. You cannot learn everything in one sitting, but if you watch regularly, your knowledge will slowly grow. The habit of watching will get you more involved, and perhaps you start researching online and in newspapers as well, to expand your knowledge. You become more comfortable with the subject matter, and you start to seek out conversations about current headlines with others, interacting, arguing, and learning in the process. This is how you become expert. It starts with a thought, but by turning the TV on, you opened a channel to the news, and you opened your mind to its knowledge.

> *For where two or three gather in my name, there am I with them.*
> *- Matthew 18:20*

We can equate church to local news programming. Church provides the structure on which to build your relationship. It gives the opportunity to practice your beliefs, away from the distractions of everyday life. Like the news broadcasts at certain times in the day, churches offer a connecting experience to believers at certain times as well.

Practice makes perfect. The repetitive action builds our relationship with God; it builds our faith and it builds our knowledge as well. It cannot happen instantly. It takes that reiteration of devotion and desire. To think that you can grow a valuable bond with God by going to your backyard tree every few months for some meditation, or praying for your team during the commercial break of the football game, is naïve and foolish. If God could be insulted, I am certain he would be. Wouldn't you?

Love must be proven.

It is not enough that I tell my wife several times a day that I love her if, when she needs me to go to the store to pick up some medicine, I just go back to reading my newspaper. If she has a cold and needs some medicine to help her sleep, I jump right up and go to the store, in the rain, to get her the medicine to relieve her discomfort.

The proof of love is in the deed, not in the language.

Language is easy. Demonstrating love takes dedication and effort. Not only do I do this to prove my love for her, I am *grateful* for the opportunity to do so. It proves my love for her *to me*.

Religion is a courtship of God.

When I get up early to go to church, it is an opportunity to show God my devotion; that I want to be with Him, to worship Him as I bring Him my physical body (that he gave me). It would be easier just to lie in bed and pray, but I revel in the chance to prove my love, as a good husband would for his wife. I also enjoy the celebration of the church service with other worshippers. The power that is created by a hundred believers worshipping together is much greater than the sum of its parts.

Because God is the all-powerful, all-knowing creator of the universe, it is impudent (and imprudent) for us to think that just praying when it is convenient to us is adequate to establish a relationship. The parent who fields calls from the college kid asking for money in the middle of the night (because that is when it is convenient for the child to call) has a right to be indignant. The child who shows his love by sending a photo, phoning on a birthday, or just to say "hi" engenders a different sort of relationship.

If I want to learn tennis, I should go to a tennis court. Just hitting tennis balls against my garage door will not improve my tennis game as much as improve my ability to hit balls against the door of a garage. The funny thing is, if I put on tennis shorts and tennis shoes, and go to the tennis court for a lesson, I feel much more the tennis player than if I were barefooted at home facing my garage door. The exercise of attending church does a wonderful thing for us: it creates in us more devotion and a greater appreciation for God.

Without the courtship, there is no growth toward the ultimate understanding of love that we are meant to experience, namely our unification with God. Without this progression, without actively pursuing a relationship with God, we are simply living out our days, leaving our souls to collect dust on a shelf. Trying to be good people is not enough to create what our souls need. Being nice to your mailman is not enough. Not cheating at golf is not enough.

On the flip-side, showing up for church will not automatically make you holy. The act of attending church is a symbolic one that has an amazing impact on your psyche, and a unique opportunity, but once inside the doors of the church, you still have free choice. You can listen to the sermon or fall asleep. You can take the message with you, or leave it (figuratively) in the pew. If you attend church simply to impress your friends or business partners, you may as well not go. God cannot be cheated, though many have tried! Your personal desire for communion with God is essential.

Reciprocity in a relationship.

If a man comes home to his wife, and he is tired and it is miserably cold out and he simply walks in, and without even saying "hi," turns on the TV, he will get one reception. But, if he goes out of his way in the cold to pick up flowers, comes in and hugs her and presents her with the flowers, her treatment of him will be a hundred percent different. In each case, he sees a return on his investment that corresponds proportionately to the intensity of his outlay. How different will his evening be once he decides to put more into it! He is greeted differently when he demonstrates his love in actions. The entire evening changes from his modified efforts. Not just her evening, but his as well. He thought first of what might make his wife happy. Then he produced it and his life became happier in the process.

If he had just come home as in the first scenario, his wife probably would have known that he loved her, and maybe even that he had thought to get her flowers, but that would not change his evening. Only actions produce the results. Then those results are projected forward, so the next time he does a similar thing, her response may be, "I have the best husband in the world!" It all grows on itself. Never buying flowers leads to never buying flowers; but getting them leads to the desire to do more. It is a long path, with opportunities every day. We get one chance after another and the more we do, the more we desire to do. And through this principle the marriage grows and does not stagnate.

If you do not have the desire to know God, you will not know Him.

Your love affair with God grows through repetition and investiture. It is driven by your desire. You must *practice* your faith. You need to research it in dedicated surroundings. Thought, in and of itself, does not create anything—action does. It is not enough to say, "I am a spiritual person." It is not enough to think, "I want a closer connection to God." Acting on the thought is the key that opens the heart to God. Acting on it repeatedly is the way to form an unbreakable bond.

> *What we are is God's gift to us.*
> *What we become is our gift to God.*
> —Eleanor Powell

Chapter 20

Why Do I Need Church?

Nourish your soul and make room for joy—sorrow will take care of itself.

The most intolerant thing in life is the truth. It is unbending. Two plus two is four, and it will never be thirteen or sixty-seven or even four and a half. Not even for your birthday. It is only ever four.

> *Beauty is Truth, Truth Beauty.*
> *—John Keats*

When you get home from a trip and you are about to open your front door, you have a truth in your hand: your key. Your key must fit exactly. It has a definite length and shape and if it is bent or changed even a slight bit, the key will not unlock the door anymore. It is not sort-of true. It is not approximate. The key must be exact. Between the precision of the key and the lock there exists a striking intolerance.

In engineering it is the same story. When building a bridge or a plane, the engineer must adhere to strict standards of truth. He cannot allow for the equations to be approximately correct, because then the bridge will fall down, or the plane out of the sky. The more he knows about construction, the more narrow-minded he becomes about the equations.

If I speak to a youngster who does not know much about history, he may think that the Second World War started sometime in the late '30s. It actually started on September 1, 1939. That is an exact date. And if somebody tells you they think it started in 1938, you will say, no, it did not start in 1938. There is a date and it was September 1, 1939.

Knowledge is intolerant of anything but the truth. Only the ignorant say, "Oh, come on, be more understanding" about thus and such; but the more you know about a subject, the less flexible you can be. Facts are funny that way. A lack of knowledge does not change the truth. A three-year-old, when asked the sum of two plus two, may insist that it is pickles, but that only reveals a need for learning. We do not blame the numbers for not adding up to pickles. We teach the toddler to count on her fingers, instead. She clearly needs assistance. All human beings need guidance, although they may grow up to disdain or resent it.

To some outsiders, or hobby-churchgoers, the teachings of a Christian church might seem too rigid. But it is only as rigid as a compass that guides a ship from England to America. The compass points only North. Even a few degrees of error on the compass might land you in Brazil instead of Boston. If the compass pointed east sometimes, and sometimes south, who knows where you might end up at the conclusion of a long journey? The compass gives the captain the orientation to steer the ship, and he relies on this information absolutely. If you observed the captain arguing with the compass, insisting that north could also be slightly more west, you might consider mutiny.

The spirit of the times is ever-changing.

Some people wish to see churches modernize. How long does modern last? There is a word in German, *zeitgeist*, which literally means time-spirit. This word can be translated as trend, although its essence is more than that. Trends are, by definition, short-lived.

They are diametrically opposed to the truth, which is everlasting. Modern is not necessarily the truth. In fact, because it is ethereal and inconsistent, in many instances the spirit of the times is absolutely wrong.

"Modern," by definition, is only temporary.

The southern states in the U.S. used to condone slavery. More than that, actually, they celebrated it. It was in the spirit of the times, but it was an evil arrangement, and thankfully, it has been abolished. Think about that. People used to sit around talking about the slave they just purchased, or how best to get the most work out of a good slave. They thought slavery was the will of God, when, of course, nothing could be further from the truth. I am sure more than a few preachers gave sermons regarding slavery, and not necessarily against it. That was the *zeitgeist*, but it did not change the *truth*. When God led Moses to demand of Pharaoh, "Let my people go," He was having Moses speak on behalf of all humans for all time. That is the unbending truth.

As early as 1435, the Catholic Pope condemned racial slavery. Fifty-seven years before Columbus discovered America, and well before the Thirteenth Amendment, the Spanish had made slavery a practice in their discovery and colonization of the Canary Islands. The Pope was determined to put an end to enslavement of any peoples, and ordered that they were to bet let free with no money exchanging hands. Any faithful who did not obey were excommunicated ipso facto. Unfortunately, the practice of slavery did not end. This is a failing of the humans, not of the Church. Although the Church may have been politically weak and unable to influence public opinion, or zeitgeist, about slavery, that by no means indicates the Church ever condoned slavery. Churches cannot stop every evil practice. They are simply a beacon, or compass. Therefore it is imperative that a church's light shines unwaveringly on the truth.

How many observe Christ's birthday! How few his precepts!
O! 'tis easier to keep holidays than commandments.
—Benjamin Franklin, Poor Richard's Almanack, 1757

Bell-bottoms and big hair used to be modern, and today we snicker at them. What if, in the seventies, church clergy adopted funk-a-delic robes and platform shoes in which to offer communion? How would that play today, do you think? "Achy-Breaky Heart," as recorded by Billy Ray Cyrus, was a number one hit in 1992. Should a church change its music to align with the times? If we recalibrate our compasses each time a new idea, fashion or song comes out, we will most certainly be floundering at sea. We will never find our destination because our direction will be constantly changing. Your church is supposed to represent the everlasting truth of God, so it may not be modern, but it must be timeless. On occasion, that means flying in the face of what is considered current or progressive thought.

Historically, the Christian church has gone through many transitions and has often adapted to the spirit of the times, the current 'morality.' Thankfully, it often has not. True North is still True North. Although it has struggled throughout its 2000 year history, it still maintains Christ's message, and you can still be saved by His Grace. If it had succumbed to the constant pressure to change, to adapt to the changing times, certainly it would not have survived at all. No worldly institution has lasted for over 2000 years or even a quarter of that time. That fact is a remarkable testament to the strength and purity of Christ's message.

The word religion comes from the Latin word religio. A common theory now is that the Latin root word derives from ligare "bind, connect." The prefixed re-ligare is interpreted as re (again) + ligare or "to reconnect." Church is intended to reconnect the soul to its maker. It maintains that the only way to do that is through Christ.

"I came to bear witness to the Truth."
—Christ's answer to Pontius Pilot.

Nobody faults the Olympic team when they say you must run the hundred meters in a certain time or less, in order to make the team. There is a standard of excellence to achieve Olympic greatness. There is also a standard of excellence for God and for His church.

We now live in a time of "tolerance," which makes almost any judgment seem too rigid. We are being conditioned to believe in moral relativity. By that, I mean that while I do not condone wife beating, in some cultures it is accepted, considered moral, and even encouraged. Therefore, relatively speaking, wife beating is okay, so I should not judge the wife beaters. During the prosecution of Michael Vick, the famous football player, for dog fighting, Whoopi Goldberg voiced on "The View" that dog fighting is a part of his culture. She said, "from where he comes from" (the South) it is more common, implying that somehow makes it okay.

Moral relativity is dangerous.

If dog fighting is a part of Vick's accepted culture (it is not, but just follow me here) should he be allowed to bring his moralities with him, and are we not to judge them, relevant to our own? For some reason, moral relativity brings outside morals into our culture and asks that we accept them as our own. In certain Muslim cultures, honor killing of a daughter who dares to date or even look at a non-Muslim boy is considered a moral imperative. Not optional, *essential* to preserving the honor of the family. The father must kill the daughter who has brought shame on his house. Moral relativity dictates that we should accept it, though this behavior is abhorrent to us. Political correctness teaches us not to criticize because it holds that everyone is entitled to his own morality.

Where, then, is the line?

I can tell you where—nowhere. Everything and any kind of outrageous behavior, as long as two or three people agree it works for them, becomes equally valuable to a society that relies on moral relativity. If a man starts a sect specifically for the raping of pre-teen girls, that is just super. The North American Man-Boy Love Association (NAMBLA) is an organization dedicated to grown men seducing young boys and using them as sex toys. There is nothing good or right with the membership in this group, but the American Civil Liberties Union (ACLU) insists we applaud them for their unique qualities and for their dedication to sexually molesting children. Clearly this line of inevitable reasoning leads to Hell on earth.

Undoubtedly, the world calls out for an indisputable moral compass by which we can judge and steer. Who or what shall serve as that compass? An independently appointed governmental coalition of bureaucrats? Hannah Montana? Michael Vick?

Morals are deliberately inflexible.

God sent us rules and morals in the Ten Commandments, which are nothing more than a very basic understanding of moral life. The people who demand that churches be more tolerant or understanding or adaptable really are insisting that God adjust to sinfulness. Unfortunately for them, it must be the other way around. Sinfulness has to adjust to God by becoming pure. That path is an extremely difficult one. That path is the reason why this earth and all its creatures exist. It is the essence of life to become God-like through an amazing and challenging spiritual journey.

Society has become all too invested in praising children un-deservedly. Once we were concerned our children were too insecure as they grew up. Our response has been to create the "me" generation.

Reportedly, our children now have too much self-esteem! Four-year-olds get trophies for playing their first season of T-ball. Picture these kids, picking daisies in the outfield and winning awards for those efforts. They may like the shiny metal, but they are confused by the accolades. Even a four-year-old knows what is undeserved. Researchers have discovered that low self-esteem is not nearly as dangerous to youth as previously thought. Astonishing. But more amazing still, the new higher self-esteem that has been successfully fostered in today's youth has apparently led to increased drug and alcohol use, narcissism, bullying, and more teenage sex, not less, as was previously assumed. When it comes to teaching children, over praising is actually worse than under praising, probably because the overly praised child has a sense of entitlement that does not serve a moral master. Things a child with low self-esteem would not do, risks he would not take, the overly praised child is more liable to try. The entitlement attitude can beat down any moral standard he may have been provided.

The piano teacher does not congratulate the student if the entire song was played incorrectly. He does not commend the child on each mistake. Instead he corrects, and encourages the child only on the correct things. Between the mistakes and proper playing the child eventually learns to play piano.

It is not the duty of the church to approve every little thing that we think would be fun for us. Christianity is there to uphold the values that God set out for us, and for it to do otherwise would be like spoiling the children of God with praise where none was earned. When you are young, you go to church and the priest tells you not to steal, not to lie, but to be a good child. When you go home, perhaps you steal or tell a lie, but if you are repeatedly exposed to the good message of the church it gets more difficult to be bad. You hear the voice of morality in your head.

A non-religious man told the following story:

He was walking in New York City down a dark alley in Harlem at midnight. Suddenly, he saw a dozen male youths in rapper clothing come out of a basement and walk toward him. He said at that point he tightened up with fear, naturally. Then, as he kept moving, he noticed the streetlight reflecting off a sign over the basement doorway that said "Midnight Bible Study." Immediately, he felt more relaxed. Why? Because we all know the message of God and the Bible is one of peace. Studying the Bible does not immediately make us good, but it is a step in the right direction. Listening to the message of purity makes us want to become more pure, and when we find others on that path, we are more at ease in the knowledge that they, too, are searching for the light and the good.

If our religion were to compromise on the truth, it would fail entirely. But church is a human institution, prone to human error. It is comprised of people who chose a different path, one without Ferraris or yachts. They said goodbye to a materialistic lifestyle, in favor of a spiritual one. They became our moral educators, and as such they must have had an intrinsic intolerance for falseness and evil. They are determined to serve as the arrow on our moral compass, pointing to True North even if we followers are not headed in that direction. All humans are flawed. Although we will try and often fail, we are forgiven and encouraged to try again. Without the moral compass, we would be unaware of our failings and we would flounder without hope.

Same great taste, now with fewer morals.

Religion-light fails, much like if you took your key to the locksmith and asked for 'sort of' a copy. Almost will not open the lock. There is one key, and no room for 'sort of.' Either it is the correct key or an exact copy, or the door stays shut. The truth is that absolute and intolerant. The Christian church is here to uphold the truth on earth. It is imperative that it stays faithful to that pursuit.

I can do a lot of things that are wrong. I can intellectually decide I want to be free and jump out of the 22nd story of a building. For the entire 12 seconds on the way down, I might enjoy my decision, before cause and effect takes hold and produces an enormous mess. It is not in the design of man to jump off buildings, without some flying aid. A Porsche is a great car, a fast car that drives like a dream, but if I try to use it as a water-ski boat … It just is not designed for that.

Just because I desire something does not make it normal or correct.

I might be born with a violent temper. Does that make it good? Of course not. Should I try to curb my vicious tendencies? Definitely, and it is possible to do so. Perhaps you were born with kleptomania. Does that mean the store you steal from should not prosecute you? "It feels right," or it is "in my blood," does not validate it or make it reasonable. Say I am born with absolutely no musical talent, but I desire to learn to play piano. If I practice religiously for the next ten or fifteen years, I will be much more musically inclined than if I had not turned in that direction.

Picture an empty vase, in the center of an enormous circle of larger urns with marbles in them. These are urns of opportunity. Some of them are good opportunities, and some are not. The marbles in each urn are different colors, indicating the degree of goodness of the choice. On one side of the circle there are mainly dark and evil marbles; and the respectable urns, with pale colored marbles, are opposite those.

You are the empty vase. Your thirst for knowledge creates a marble shoot to the urn of your choice. If you want to learn French, the French urn tips marbles into your vase. If you try learning tennis, marbles come down the shoot from the tennis urn. We are constantly collecting marbles. Some of them are good and some are bad. If you tell someone a nasty lie about your boss, a dark marble flows into your vase. Compliment someone on his or her creativity and a pale marble drops in. It is up to you to choose which marble to invite into your vase. Some people bend more easily to one side or another. If they choose the dark side, it will fill them up, whereas those who turn to God, Truth, and Love, will be filled with those qualities. Undoubtedly, Pol Pot, Mao, and Hitler, each turned toward the dark side. You cannot perpetrate such evil acts and not have drunk your fill from those urns. Their vases are replete with dark, cloudy marbles. And those people could not have accomplished all of that evil alone; they lured others to join them. Perhaps they knew what they were involved in, perhaps initially not. But once they turned toward those urns, the marbles flowed in. And the problem was, with so many marbles coming from that side, fewer 'good' marbles could hope to fit in there.

Most people try a few marbles out of many different urns, and have a mix of various colors in their vases. The desire would be to get as light as possible, and then light flows to you as well. The opposite is true also. The downward spiral of evil encourages more and more evil. It all begins with thought. Choose what you think with care, because as you think it, you build the shoots for the marbles, and they will flow.

God forgives all your sins. He understands that humans will fail, just like a child will fail as he learns to play a violin. But at the same time, church cannot sanction something that goes against nature, or God, just to be more pleasing or less aggravating to a few. Tolerance can happen outside of truth, but the truth does not permit contradiction, and our churches are here to uphold that standard and keep us on course.

No God, no peace.
Know God, know peace.
—Author Unknown

Chapter 21

Why Should I Pray?

Pray as though everything depended on God.
Work as though everything depended on you.
—Saint Augustine

We have discussed how this world is not real in the way we experience it. Our reality is illusion. We are not matter, as much as energy. We have covered the power of thought, the initiating source of everything. What is prayer, if not thought? What are thoughts, if not the beginning? We pray because that is where we begin. We instigate our relationship with our creator, and start a reciprocating connection.

We discover ourselves in prayer, just as we discover God.

A friend once interrogated me on the merits of prayer. The point he tried to make is that a whole monastery of monks praying in seclusion about a subject could never equal the potential that might be realized should those same monks participate in society and actually *do*. They waste their time thinking about life's tragedies and praying about them, instead of building a hospital or a school or administering vaccines somewhere.

Why don't they stop praying and start doing?

Most of us live in the real world, with our cars and construction companies, trains and busses and hospitals. We interact and conduct business. A software engineer who is devoted to his work basically lives in his cubical, designing programs or other equally intangible products. What, exactly, is he *doing*? It looks like nothing.

But is it nothing, just because to the outsider, to someone unfamiliar with computers, or someone uneducated in how computers work, it seems like so much drivel?

The software changes everything. Computers could not run without it and no plane would fly without it as well. Trains would collide, hospitals would not function, even your phone would not work without the software that runs the computer.

Just because sitting at a computer terminal typing and thinking and manipulating and running tests seems like a useless endeavor to an ignorant observer, does not make it so.

Prayer is the software.

Coming back to those useless monks who sit around praying all day … There is more to prayer than meets the eye. By praying, we have an opportunity to alter the software code. We get into the deepest part of what regulates us and have the chance thereby to change the screen. Prayer, the admission of and submission to a higher source, connects us to our maker via the hardwiring we are born with.

Reach out and touch someone, with prayer.

If I ask you if you and your mother are close, you may answer, "Oh, yes, very close. I spoke to her four years ago." If you only spoke to her four years ago, then by definition you have no relationship with your mother, and if you last spoke with her six months ago the same holds true. Only if you desire a connection with her will you forge that relationship you claim, by contacting her, informing her of what is going on in your life, visiting her, and doing things for her. Saying you have a relationship, and having the relationship are two different things. You must invite her into your life, and have her open hers to you, in order to sustain a true relationship.

Through prayer we form our relationship to God.

A few years ago, Peter Jennings and ABC nightly news ran a special on religion and prayer. The first segment investigated a scientific study in which researchers infected a group of 40 mice with cancerous tumor cells. The mice were separated into a test group and a control group. In the control group all the infected mice died within 21 days. The test group was prayed over by people of the cloth as well as lab workers. With the exception of 2 mice that lived, all the others died as well, but only after 60 days. This study scientifically demonstrated the power of prayer. It is not necessarily a quantifiable power, but it is certainly qualitative. In this case, of course, the mice were not aware of prayer so the well-known placebo effect (that patients feel better because they know people are praying for them,) exerted no influence in this experiment.

The second segment of the show dealt with a woman whose brain had been completely mapped out for study. Using magnetic resonance imaging, MRI, while they asked her to think of certain things or emotions, the researchers distinctly documented each area of the brain that the woman used. For example, when she thought of love, a certain part of her brain lit up on the MRI, but when she was afraid a different area was active. When she was angry, yet another region glowed. In all of their machinations, there was one part of the woman's brain that lay dormant. No matter what emotions the woman was put through, this particular section of her brain had no light, or visible activity. Until she prayed. Only then would this part be energized. This seems to prove that we are hardwired to call our maker, as if we have a red phone with a direct line.

> *God speaks in the silence of the heart.*
> *Listening is the beginning of prayer.*
> *—Mother Teresa*[17]

The third segment of Jennings' show explained results of a study concluding, in general, that people who pray and attend religious services on a regular basis live longer than people who do not. I admit that this result surprised even me. On average, a praying person's life expectancy is nine and one-half years longer than one who does not pray. The simplest reason, which is itself a complex subject, is *hope*. People who go to church believe there is a higher power, and that He is good. People who pray have optimism and are less likely to give up. Perhaps prayerful people have hope, which allows them happiness and the will to live. Prayer simply helps people overcome hardship better than a lack of belief.

> *Certain thoughts are prayers.*
> *There are moments when, whatever be the*
> *attitude of the body, the soul is on its knees.*
> *—Victor Hugo*

My father was diagnosed with bladder cancer when he was 62. The cancer had spread and the prognosis was very pessimistic. My family met with the surgeon and he explained the next steps that had to be taken. The operation was risky, my father would likely lose a lot of blood, and the state of the cancer was too widespread for my father to have much hope. That night our family prayed together like never before. We also asked Christ to keep our beloved father safe during the operation and, of course, that God's will be done.

> *I have been driven many times to my knees by the*
> *overwhelming conviction that I had nowhere else to go.*
> *—Abraham Lincoln*

I will never forget the surgeon and his emotions after the operation. He began by calmly stating that everything went well and that my father was recovering. Then, with a perplexed grin he told us that he could not explain the incredible results of the surgery. Our father, completely contrary to expectations, had hardly lost any blood. He showed us the images of the cancerous tissues from before and after the operation, which were taken only two days apart. It was as if they were from a different person. Only a small percentage of the cancerous tissue remained on the post operation images and my father, after his original death sentence, lived another decade and every day of that we considered a blessing.

What happened?

Well, obviously the surgeon did his job very well. But even he admitted there was some other 'magic' in the air.

> *Call on God, but row away from the rocks.*
> *—Indian Proverb*

Synchronicity.

Praying has many forms. I can pray at home or on a mountaintop. Of course God is everywhere, but Christ also said that where three or more are gathered He will be in their midst. The sum of the parts is more than the parts by themselves. When we go to a church service and we pray with 200 people the power together is a whole lot greater than when we sit on a tree stump in the woods and pray. That is why people have forever assembled to pray. The words, "Let us pray together," have not been spoken billions of times because we are too lonely to pray by ourselves but because together we attain a resonance that inspires and moves us. Synchronicity.

How should I pray?

> *Our Father, who art in heaven,*
> *Hallowed be thy Name.*
> *Thy kingdom come.*
> *Thy will be done,*
> *On earth as it is in heaven.*
> *Give us this day our daily bread.*
> *And forgive us our trespasses,*
> *As we forgive those who trespass against us.*
> *And lead us not into temptation,*
> *But deliver us from evil.*
> *[For thine is the kingdom,*
> *and the power, and the glory,*
> *forever and ever.]*
> *Amen.*

The Lord's Prayer is probably the best, most succinct prayer ever written. It covers just about everything regarding praying and living. It is our red phone line, direct to God.

In this prayer, "Thy will be done," tells us exactly who is in charge, and points out all exists and is done by the grace of God. "Bread" refers to everything humans need: food, clothing, air, breath, water, heat, everything. Our sustenance.

When at night you cannot sleep,
talk to the Shepherd and stop counting sheep.
—Author Unknown

The most important part of the Lord's Prayer, if there may be one, is in the two lines about forgiveness. This is the crux of Christian teaching and what we often find most difficult to practice. That is precisely why Jesus included it in such a way in His prayer. "As we forgive those who trespass against us." How can I ask for forgiveness while I harbor resentment in my heart? It is hypocritical. Jesus taught you to remove the plank from your own eye before attempting to get the splinter out of someone else's. Isn't that the truth? We often are so quick to criticize others for the things we are, ourselves, guilty of!

Prayer requires more of the heart than of the tongue.
—Adam Clarke

The Lord's Prayer is the simplest way to start praying, and for this reason it has endured through the millennia. It serves to guide us in our supplications and our gratitude to our heavenly Father. But prayer is a very personal matter. It can be short or long, happy or sad. It can be in your own words, or a repetition of others'. It can be on your knees, in a church, or lying prostrate on the floor of your closet. You may speak it aloud, or say it silently in your head. It can be on any subject matter. He knows them all.

Types of prayer:
  1. Supplication
  2. Intercessory
  3. Grateful

Praying is formulating your love for God, showing God you have set this time away for Him and that you want Him to be in your life on a regular basis. The more we pray the more we open a door into the infinite dimension of the spiritual. But as Christ stipulated with the Lord's Prayer, you must pray with an unburdened heart. This means that you must forgive those who have wronged you, so that you might ask for forgiveness yourself. He was specific in this instruction.

Lord, please help me ...

> *Pray, and let God worry.*
> *—Martin Luther*

Supplicating prayer is asking for help. Christ reminds us repeatedly that we are not to be anxious, but to set our worries at God's feet. One way of doing this is to pray about your troubles. Pray with the knowledge that God hears you and cares about you. Pray that He gives you the answer, and know His answers are *good*. They may not be your answers, but they will do for you.

Lord, please help my friend ...

> *There is something in humility which strangely exalts the heart.*
> *—Saint Augustine*

Intercessory prayer is the kind that they always ask for in church. "Please write down prayer requests and put them in the collection baskets." "We have our prayer chain standing by." Intercessory prayer is amazing, because it involves people who may not even know each other praying for each other. We pray that God intercedes on someone else's behalf. We pray selflessly. It raises us up while humbling us. It is a blessed thing to do.

Lord, I thank you ...

Gratitude is not only the greatest of virtues,
but the parent of all the others.
—Cicero

We are here by God's grace; meaning that without God, none of what you are and have is possible. You should thank God for everything. I often start with the most trivial or overlooked issues when I pray my grateful prayers. I thank God for the sheets on my bed, for the spoon I eat with, for my hands. I am grateful for my fax machine and a computer that works (usually). I thank him for the health of my children and my friends, and for my own health. I thank Him for all His generosity in my life and for His continued support. The grateful prayer can be a kind of meditation. The most powerful effect of the grateful prayer is that in thanking God, you become more appreciative of the gifts in your life, and you more readily recognize how "lucky" you are. This is very successful in changing your perspective. It can effectively lesson your burdens by contrasting them with what you already have achieved. Try it; it works.

It is all a gift.

Prayer is the gift God gave us; our chance to call him whenever we wish. We are hardwired in our brains to converse with him. He never sleeps or asks us to call back in ten minutes. He is never too busy to chat. His promise is to be there for us to guide us through this experience called life. Even Christ Himself, the Son of God, prayed. Better than that, he wrote the book on it.

Instead of asking God to heal your heart, pray that you may heal His.

Open your heart to prayer, and open your heart to God. Ask God to dwell in your heart, and ask him to reveal to you His answers. Understand and acknowledge that He will. God loves you, His creation, His child, with all of His heart. He wants what is best for you, but He cannot act without your invitation. Send it "return receipt requested."

> *He who created us without our help*
> *will not save us without our consent.*
> *—Saint Augustine*

Afterword

No good deed goes unpunished ...

In the body of this book we have explored the scientific and metaphysical elements of nature that explain and illustrate a higher power, the creator, God. While all the laws of the universe bind all of us, cause and effect is the law most relevant to human emotions. It is a law of accountability. We are living in a time of reduced answerability because we have strayed from God and this law. Our society has slowly been seduced by materialism, away from the spiritual plane, and away from the obvious truth of the inevitable cycle of causation and consequence.

You cannot escape yourself. Jesus taught the principle of reciprocity—what you sow you will reap. This is unavoidable, so the sooner you accept it, the better off you will be in the long run. There is no guilt-free sin. Everything you do effects at least one person: you.

Unfortunately, some Christians spend a lot of time trying not to be accountable. Superficially, the teachings of Christianity can be interpreted to mean if you commit a sin, all you need to do is own up to it in the eyes of the Lord, and He forgives you. It's like an all-events pass. Go where you want, do what you want, then set it straight with God later, and you are golden. Does that make sense? Of course not. There is the mafia's Christianity, where they attend church and tithe regularly and generously, but in their business life they are doing all sorts of improper, illegal, and immoral activities, for which they repent in the confessional and are absolved of guilt. Hypocritical? You bet. Ridiculously illogical? Absolutely.

Any Christian who takes his faith seriously believes in <u>absolute</u> accountability. Our faith is in a forgiving God, a God who knows all too well that we are human, and that sinning and forgiving is all part of our learning experience.

Lucifer rebelled because he wanted to *be* God. Being an angel, with God, was not enough for him. Some people want to be God in their own lives but that is a trap. They are ostensible Christians instead of spiritual, performing for the cameras, when their spirits are not decidedly for God. They may project and imitate Christ outwardly, but harbor resentment and petty jealousy in their hearts. They try to justify their transgressions, apologize for them afterward, but understand, please, that the payments for those misguided actions are put on account.

ACCOUNTABLITY

You are not judged by God …

You judge yourself (at least you should,) and justice metes out your sentence, unconditionally and appropriately, as the law of balance requires. You are ruled by cause and effect and your own deeds. All your actions come back to you, not because of a vengeful God, but because of a relentless and impartial logic that drives the universe.

The good news …

We are conditioned to run from responsibility, in general and as a society. Responsibility is *hard*. But that knee-jerk reaction is foolish. There is great relief to be found in responsibility and accountability.

Remember the first time you rode your bike? Your dad took off the training wheels, pushed you forward down the sidewalk, and then suddenly you noticed he wasn't there anymore, and you were riding all by yourself. He had helped, but as you rode around, you understood that you were in charge, and it was a freeing, exhilarating moment. Was it hard to do? Was it scary? Of course, but daddy was there encouraging you and helping you, and you took the handles in your own two hands and off you went. When you turned the bike around and rode back to your driveway, you were a changed kid. You took ownership of that bike, and of that empowering emotion. You were in control, driving, just like today you can choose to drive your life.

Like riding a bike ...

Though it may seem like a burden, there is relief in bearing responsibility. Take possession of your life, because your soul is the only thing you really have right now. You may do it mechanically at first, simply by acknowledging your involvement even in circumstances that initially might have seemed out of your control. That takes practice. Start by refusing to see yourself as the victim. Understand that you are always the creator of your perceptions and your environment. Fight the urge to surrender your power and perceive yourself as a slave to circumstance. That is the option of weakness. You are not a slave. God would not wish that for you. *You* control your choices, always.

You are not the victim of your choices; you are the product of them.

Once you become accustomed to that neutral position of command, you can then move past it into a mature freedom. This is where effortless grace enters your life. After practicing the choice of happiness, you become more adept at applying happiness in your life. This comes not from shirking responsibility, but by owning it. Yes, you are in control of your own universe, and there is a great freedom in that. Once you can embrace that, you are truly free to give and to love generously and unreservedly.

> *As fire when thrown into water is cooled down and put out, so also a false accusation when brought against a man of the purest and holiest character, boils over and is at once dissipated, and vanishes ...*
> —*Marcus Tullius Cicero*

If someone insults you, but you are versed in this principle, their insults bounce off you, because they are the owners of that aggression, and you recognize that you only do harm to yourself by accepting it into your life. Reject the aggression, deny it access to your heart, meet it with kindness and understanding, and you are free. Grace can blossom in the absence of hatred and resentment in your heart. If you harbor resentment, forgive yourself and the person you resent. If you have no resentment, what is there to forgive? Dispel resentment. It is only useful for increasing suffering.

The choice of grace.

There is a cycle to anger. Joe fails a test of the spirit by betraying his sister, Jenny. Jenny gets angry and yells at Joe. Then Joe is upset and hurts Jenny even more, and the anger and hostility escalate until everyone is exhausted, even me, and I'm only writing about it. Imagine a different scenario. Joe failed the test and told Jenny's secret to Ed. Jenny hears about it. Why did she tell Joe her secret? That was her *choice*. Jenny goes to Joe and says, "Joe, we had an agreement, and you betrayed me. But I never should have shared my secret with you. That was selfish and stupid of me. I forgive you." Then she goes to Ed and says, "I am sorry that Joe told you this thing, and now you are burdened by it. You had a choice to listen or not, and now I ask you to choose not to share this information. It is my fault the secret is out, but you're responsible for it now." Ed thinks about it and decides it's really none of his business, so he tries to forget the secret, and it dies there. Joe repents, apologizes, and takes responsibility for his part in this, and peace reigns. Jenny short-circuited the anger cycle with *grace*. So did Ed, and Joe. If everyone lived with grace, there would be an end to anger.

Don Miguel Ruiz, author of "The Four Agreements," summarized this principle in his book. He recommends the reader make this agreement *with himself*:

> *Don't take anything personally …*
> *When you are immune to the opinions and actions of others*
> *you won't be the victim of needless suffering.*
> *—Don Miguel Ruiz*

It is challenging, at first, to learn to live this way; but ultimately it is *empowering*. Try it! *You have the control.* The next time someone gets under your skin, imagine simply that they have their (very good) reasons. After all, you have no idea, honestly, what demons they are battling. Another of the four agreements is to not make assumptions. Assumptions can kill grace. Understand that most people's lives are assumptive, though they needn't be. The rest is the perception you apply to those assumptions. Choose nurturing assumptions, if any, which bring peace. Apply your own perceptions to any situation, and take authority for your life. Grace everyone with love and disengage from evil in every form. It will get easier over time.

Resist not evil, but overcome it with good.

This is a call to arms. By taking responsibility for your own life, for your choices, you lose the illusion of vulnerability, and you gain autonomy. It may be frightening at first, but it is worth it in the end. Think about this. When you take ownership of your life, you become responsible: *able to respond*. Your status as a victim is abolished and you can fully react to others around you. Taking on your accountability *enables* you to live a more complete life because you are accepting power over your life. Rejecting accountability is a rejection of that same power and a renunciation of freedom. You cannot have it both ways. Placing your personal responsibilities on someone else enslaves you, but cherishing them empowers you to live, to love, and to be happy. And when you are happy and loving to yourself and to others, you make the world a better place.

> *I never look at the masses as my responsibility; I look at the individual. I can only love one person at a time—just one, one, one. So you begin. I began—I picked up one person. Maybe if I didn't pick up that one person, I wouldn't have picked up forty-two thousand ... The same thing goes for you, the same thing in your family, the same thing in your church, your community. Just begin—one, one, one.*
> —Mother Teresa[18]

Footnotes

1   From "Physics and Reality" in *Journal of the Franklin Institute* 221, no. 3, March 1936.

2   Robert Jastrow. *God and the Astronomers*, p. 116. Readers Library ISBN-10: 0393850064

3   "Science, Philosophy, and Religion," Einstein's contribution to a symposium, 1940

4   *A Brief History of Time*, Steven Hawking, New York: Bantam, 1998. P. 126

5   Einstein's answer to Frank Wall, New York, 1933

6   www.merriam-webster.com/dictionaryreincarnation"> reincarnation</a>

7   From the essay, "Optimism", 1903

8   Letter to Cornelius Lanczos March 21,1942

9   *Savitri, A Legend and a Symbol.* Pondicherry: Sri Aurobindo Ashram, 1970.

10   www.merriam-webster.com/dictionary/resonate>

11   The Heritage Foundation; How Poor are America's Poor? Examining the "Plague" of poverty in America, by Robert Rector, August 27, 2007

12   From a letter to Olga Lee, January 16,1954

13   *The Way to Love: Meditations for Life.* New York: Image, 2012

14   *Teaching About Evolution and the Nature of Science.* Washington, DC: National Academy of Sciences, 1998, p. 58

15   As recalled by Prince Hubertus zu Loewenstein. Quoted in his autobiography Towards the Further Shore, 1968.

16   Encarta® World English Dictionary © 1999 Microsoft Corporation.

17   The writings of Mother Teresa of Calcutta © by the Mother Teresa Center, exclusive licensee throughout the world of the Missionaries of Charity for the works of Mother Teresa. Used with permission.

18   The writings of Mother Teresa of Calcutta © by the Mother Teresa Center, exclusive licensee throughout the world of the Missionaries of Charity for the works of Mother Teresa. Used with permission.

CPSIA information can be obtained at www.ICGtesting.com
Printed in the USA
LVOW08s1639310314

379675LV00002B/715/P